Ready, Set, Roll!

Number Cube Games

25 Fun, Easy-to-Play Games That Build Key Math Skills

by Lorraine Hopping Egan

SCHOLASTIC
PROFESSIONAL BOOKS

New York ▫ Toronto ▫ London ▫ Auckland ▫ Sydney

■□

To Jan,
who's always game
for learning fun
—*L. H. E.*

Cover design by Jaime Lucero and Vincent Ceci

Cover illustration by Michael Moran

Interior design by Ellen Matlach Hassell
for Boultinghouse & Boultinghouse, Inc.

Interior illustration by Michael Moran and Manuel Rivera

ISBN 0-590-18736-8

Copyright © 1998 by Lorraine Hopping Egan.

Contents

Introduction

Number Cube Games in Your Classroom

Every game in this book aims to please—to please educators by teaching skills, to please kids by being fun! Far from being Friday afternoon filler, these games provide hard-core practice in computation, problem solving, logical thinking, understanding probability, applying geometry, and much more.

While you and your students are having so much fun learning, you'll be in some very serious company. Using dice to analyze math problems was a near obsession for such deep thinkers as Leonardo da Vinci, Galileo, Sir Isaac Newton, Blaise Pascal, and a host of ancient Greek and Roman philosophers.

As these geniuses knew well, the purpose of rolling dice is to generate random numbers, an excellent reason to use them in an elementary math class. The colorful dice included with this book are all you need to play a variety of number games. When combined with household objects such as buttons and beads, the dice become an even more powerful teaching tool. (See Handy Materials, right.) You'll also find reproducible rule sheets, score sheets, and game boards throughout the book.

Most of the games are very simple; show students how to play, and they're off and learning. Some games benefit from adult interpretation and supervision. Only one game (Lotto Factor-y) depends on it.

Lotto Factor-y is also a good example of a game that can include the whole class or just a small group of players. You'll also find games for one player, two players, and up to six players in a group. Why six? Because in my experience, six plays is about as long as most children will wait patiently for their turn. While it might be tempting to add extra players, I recommend keeping the groups small (two to four is ideal) and the game play fast and fun.

HANDY MATERIALS TO MAKE THE GAMES EVEN EASIER

These items will help players roll the dice fairly, follow the rules more easily, and keep score more accurately. They are necessary for a few games (indicated at the top of each rule sheet) but optional for most of the games. Game boards and other graphics are included on reproducibles. The generic reproducible score sheet on page 70 works well for several games.

- **Counters** help keep score. They show who's ahead at a glance and allow players to trade points back and forth. If you don't have a set of plastic counters in your classroom, use any small, uniform set of objects such as bottle caps, toothpicks, beads, dried beans, tiddly-winks, paper clips (big ones are worth 5 points, little ones are worth 1 point), pebbles, marbles, packing peanuts, or washers.

- **Place Markers** are playing pieces that children move around a board to mark their progress. Borrow a few from old board games or use any small objects that lie flat and can be made to look distinct for each player. In a pinch, use extra dice that are otherwise not needed in the game.

- **Dice Cups** make dice easier to handle, especially if children have to roll three or four at a time. They also give more random results and eliminate any "fudged" dice rolls. Use any opaque cup that children can completely cover with one hand.

- **Calculators** help children check answers and tabulate scores faster. As a backup to paper-and-pencil figuring, they can solve disputes instantly. Another benefit is that they can make a game that requires advanced computation playable for younger children.

Who Goes First?
Math Mini-Games Help You Decide!

These mini-games are mathematical methods for choosing who goes first. The first player is indicated as Player 1 in the rules for each game. Game play continues to his or her left in a clockwise direction.

Are the following mini-games fair, giving each player an equal chance to win? Why or why not? Do they rely on skill, luck, or both? Encourage children to invent their own "who goes first" games using dice or other random generating devices such as spinners and decks of cards.

TWO PLAYERS

- One player calls "odd" or "even." The other player rolls a die. If the caller guessed correctly, he or she goes first.

- One player flips a coin while the other calls "heads" or "tails." If the coin lands with the caller's side up, he or she goes first.

- One player hides a die in one hand and then holds out both fists. The other player taps a fist. If the fist has the die, the tapper goes first.

Alea jacta est! *

MORE THAN TWO PLAYERS

- Each player rolls a die at the same time. The highest roller goes first. If two players tie for the lead, they roll again—and again, if necessary, until one is the winner.

- Players place three dice in an opaque cup. One player shakes the cup and flips it over on the table, trapping the dice inside. Each player guesses the sum of the numbers showing on the hidden dice. The player closest to the actual sum without going over it goes first.

- Place a pile of 15 to 20 counters (toothpicks, beads, washers, etc.) in the center of the playing area. Each player takes one counter in turn until the pile is gone. The player who takes the last counter goes first.

- Players take turns drawing either one or two counters from a pile of 15 to 20 counters. (The players can draw counters in order of their birthdays.) The player to take the last counter goes first.

- Each player takes three counters and secretly hides either one, two, or all three in a fist. Players guess how many total counters are in all the players' fists. The player whose guess is closest to the actual total goes first.

- Each player takes a die and secretly turns up a number. Players reveal their numbers at the same time. The player whose number is *second* highest goes first. If the second highest number is a tie, do it again.

*The die is cast!

Zulu Dice Throw

SKILLS AND TOPICS:
- Numbers
- Addition
- Palindromes

The Game in a Nutshell

Players roll three dice and use addition to calculate their "fortunes."

Teaching Tips

The Zulu people of South Africa have an ancient tradition of telling fortunes with bones. A fortune-teller throws a set of numbered bones along with a special bone that stands for a topic—woman, man, warrior, home, or cattle (meaning wealth). The person's fate depends on luck (which numbered bones fall closest to the special bone) and on simple addition. The fortune-teller adds the numbered bones closest to the topic bone (6 + 7 = 13, for example) and looks up the sum on a numbered list of fates.

Zulu Dice Throw involves a similar "bone toss" with dice. Players roll two pairs of dice. They add the first pair to find their topics and the second pair to find their fortunes. Before playing, have students write a question for each "fortune-teller" topic on the chart: *Will I go to camp this summer?* (travel) *Will I be rich?* (wealth) *How will I do in tomorrow's soccer match?* (sports) The goal is to see if and how the Zulu bones (the dice) answer these questions.

Do the fortunes make sense? Do students believe them? (Note that many of the "fortunes" are general statements that apply in many situations.) *Which "fortunes" can you control or change by your own actions?* [Answers will vary. The idea is to help empower students to take charge of their own futures.]

Math Strategy

Do all the fortunes and topics come up equally? Why or why not? [There are more ways to roll a 7 than a 2 with two dice, for example.]

◘ MORE WAYS TO PLAY ◘

PALINDROME BONES

Players find their fortunes by turning the dice throws into palindromes: numbers such as 343 whose digits read the same forward and backward. The operation is simple: Roll the dice and make a three- or four-digit number. Reverse the digits and add the new number to the original number until you get a palindrome:

Roll	663
Backward	+ 366
	1029
	+ 9201
	10230
	+03201
Palindrome	13431

The two outside numbers are the topic (1); the inside number or numbers are the fortune (both 3 and 4 apply). Renumber the charts so that the Topic Chart starts with 1 and the Fortune Chart starts with 0.

OTHER NUMBER COMBINATIONS

By rolling three digits (for example, 1, 2, 3), how many three-digit numbers could a player make? What strategies would students use to answer this question? A few approaches:

- Roll the dice and list all the possibilities by trial and error.
- List or diagram them systematically or according to a plan (example: 123, 132, 213, 231, 312, 321, 111, 222, 333).
- Multiply the number of digits—three—by the number of place values they can occupy—also three.

How does the order of the three digits affect the fortune? Have students roll the dice, list each possible three-digit number, and calculate their fortune for each one.

Zulu Dice Throw

Any number of players

You will need: 4 dice ◻ scrap paper and pencil ◻ calculator (optional)

Winning in a Nutshell

You can't lose!
Just throw the dice.
Then compute your fortune.

The Way to Play

1. Player 1 rolls two dice and adds them. The sum is your topic. (See Topic Chart below.)

Roll: $3 + 4 = 7$

Topic: Birthdays

2. Player 1 rolls the other two dice and adds them. The sum is your fortune. (See Fortune Chart below.) The fortune applies to the topic.

Roll: $4 + 1 = 5$

Fortune: Believe in yourself and you will be happy.

3. Other players take a turn in order. Start with the player on Player 1's left.

TOPIC CHART	FORTUNE CHART
2. School	2. Look for a lucky turn of events.
3. Family	3. Think positively and everything will go fine!
4. Friends	4. A kind person is about to help you. Be thankful.
5. Holidays	5. Believe in yourself and you will be happy.
6. Travel	6. Don't let small things stand in your way.
7. Birthdays	7. Forget "don't" and "can't." Say "do" and "can."
8. Home	8. Be adventuresome. Try something new.
9. Wealth	9. Expect a surprise.
10. Health	10. Do the right thing. You can't go wrong!
11. Sports	11. What you think will happen, will happen.
12. Activities	12. Close your eyes and make a wish. Only you can make it true.

Ready, Set, Roll! Number Cube Games Scholastic Professional Books

X-Ray Vision

SKILLS AND TOPICS:
- Number Patterns
- Simple Addition
- Mental Math
- Algebraic Thinking
- Problem-Solving Strategy

The Game in a Nutshell

Players roll the dice and name the numbers on the **bottom** of the dice as fast as they can. Those who discover a pattern will win every time.

Teaching Tips

This game is called X-Ray Vision because some players seem to be able to see right through the dice. In reality, these players have found a pattern common to all standard dice: The numbers on opposite sides always add up to 7 (1 + 6, 2 + 5, 3 + 4). Based on this pattern, they can name the number on the bottom of a die in an instant.

To play, a Game Master (non-player) rolls either one, two, three, or four dice (depending on level of difficulty). Two to four players compete to name the number on the *bottom* of the die (for single-die games) or to name the sum of the numbers on the bottoms of the dice (for two- to four-dice games). Score 1 point per round won.

You could present the game as a magic trick, claiming that you can see through dice. After a few demonstrations of your "power," have children split into groups and examine a die to figure out how you did it. They write their best explanation in a sentence or two, which you can collect and discuss.

Math Strategy

When players reach the highest level—adding the bottoms of four dice—challenge them to discover another shortcut: The sum of the top and bottom combined (using four dice) is always 28:

    4 5 6 2 = 17 (top sum)
    3 2 1 5 = 11 (bottom sum)
    11 + 17 = 28

Begin by asking students to roll the dice and total the tops and bottoms separately, as in the example. Challenge them to look for patterns. *What is the highest possible roll with four dice?* [24] *What is the lowest?* [4] *When the top is showing the highest roll (all 6's), what is on the bottom dice?* [all 1's]

After students have figured out the pattern, ask: *Why 28? What is special about this number?* [28 is a product of 7 and 4—the opposite-sides sum and the number of dice.] *How can this information help you play X-Ray Vision?* [Instead of adding the hidden numbers on the bottom, they can add the top numbers and subtract the sum from 28.]

▫ MORE WAYS TO PLAY ▫

X-RAY PLACE VALUE

Assign a place value for each color of four dice: red = thousands, green = hundreds, yellow = tens, white = ones. The challenge is to look at the four digits on the tops of the dice and then name the four-digit number on the bottoms of the dice. For example, a roll of red 4, green 5, yellow 1, white 6 (4,516) corresponds to a bottom roll of 3,261. Encourage children to practice both writing and saying the numbers. If they are having difficulty, eliminate the red die for a few rounds.

Catherine and Napoleon

SKILLS AND TOPICS:
- **Inequalities**
- **Medians**
- **Problem-Solving Strategy**

The Game in a Nutshell

Players try to guess the other player's hidden dice roll based on "higher" or "lower" clues.

Teaching Tips

Catherine II of Russia (1729–1796) was Great. Her moniker said so. But just how great was she on a scale of, say, 2 to 12 (the range of possible sums using two dice)? That's what players hope to find out in the Catherine and Napoleon game. Where does Napoleon I (1769–1821) fit in? He was France's vertically challenged "Little Corporal." In the game, saying "Napoleon" means "the target number is less than your guess." Saying "Catherine" means "the number is greater than your guess."

If players make a mistake or accidentally reveal a number, simply stop the game and start over. To keep dice rolls secret, either set up a screen (a pile of books) or use dice cups. With dice cups, children can shake the dice and flip the cup upside down, trapping the dice inside. They lift the cup just enough to see the roll and then leave the dice trapped inside until the end of the game.

Math Strategy

The math strategy is simple but not always obvious to children. They should always guess the number halfway between the lowest possible number and the highest possible one. Even if the guess is wrong, they'll eliminate half of the possible numbers each turn. With this strategy, they can guess the opponent's number in four turns or fewer. (How many turns could it take if they guess at random?) Example:

Guess: 7
Result: Napoleon
Guess: 4 (8 to 12 are out; only 2 to 6 remain)
Result: Napoleon
Guess: 2 (2 and 3 are the only numbers left)

Result: Catherine
Guess: 3 (the only number left)

What other strategies do players discover? Which numbers appear most often in the game? The chapter on probability goes into more detail on this question, but students may discover that 7 is most likely to appear, followed by 6 and 8. This fact makes the "guess half" tactic even more effective.

▫ MORE WAYS TO PLAY ▫

CATHERINE TIMES NAPOLEON

Players guess the product of the two dice. The products won't include every number from 1 to 36. Part of the game is knowing which numbers to exclude. Children can make a 6 × 6 multiplication table to find out.

×	1	2	3	4	5	6
1	1	2	3			
2	2	4	6			
3	3	6				
4						
5						
6						

The missing numbers are: 7, 11, 13, 14, 17, 19, 21–23, 26–29, 31–35. *What do many of these numbers have in common?* [Many are prime numbers over 6—the highest number on a die. Many are multiples of 7, which is not on a die. There are more missing numbers as the values increase.] Have students organize the numbers by frequency. *Which numbers are least likely?* [1 and 36] *What is the halfway point?* [23 and 26 are the middle numbers.]

Catherine and Napoleon

2 players

You will need: 4 dice ▫ 20 counters or scrap paper
(to keep score) ▫ 2 dice cups (optional)

Winning in a Nutshell

Guess the number that the
other player has rolled.

The Way to Play

1. Place four counters in the center of the table. Put the others in a
pile off to the side.

2. Each player rolls two dice in secret. The sum of the dice is your
secret number.

3. Players take turns guessing each other's secret number.
(Player 1 makes the first guess.)

4. If a player guesses wrong, the other player says either "Catherine" or "Napoleon." Catherine means that the secret number is
greater than the guessed number. Napoleon means that the
secret number is less than the guessed number.

> **Player 2's secret number:** 9
>
> **Player 1 guesses:** 5
>
> **Player 2 says:** Catherine (9 is *greater than* 5)
>
> **Player 2 guesses:** 7
>
> **Player 1 says:** Napoleon (secret number is 3, *less than* 7)

5. A round ends when each player has made a guess. After each
round, remove one counter and put it back in the pile.

6. Whoever guesses the other player's secret number first wins the
counters left in the center.

7. Player 2 starts the next game. Again, place four counters in the
center. Secretly roll. Then start guessing!

Ready, Set, Roll! Number Cube Games Scholastic Professional Books

11

Poison Dice

SKILLS AND TOPICS:
- Addition
- Mental Math
- Probability

The Game in a Nutshell
Players roll four dice, pluck out any that are "poison" (1 or 6), and add the remaining dice to their scores. They roll, pluck, and score until all dice have been "poisoned." The high scorer wins.

Teaching Tips

This simple game gives children an opportunity to add columns of single-digit numbers (and an occasional two-digit number) in their heads. Players can double-check their brain power with paper and pencil or a calculator.

Here's a quick mental math tip for students to practice: In your mind, group together numbers that add up to 10 (or a multiple of 10). Add these easy numbers first. Then add the remaining numbers starting with the larger ones. Here's a typical Poison Dice score: 14, 8, 6, 3. Mentally, group the 14 and 6 for a subtotal of 20. Add 8 + 20 to get 28. Then add 28 + 3 to get 31. Encourage children to share other strategies.

Math Strategy

Discuss students' game results. *How many rolls do players make on average? What are the extremes (high and low number of rolls) per turn? Are you likely to roll a poison die on the first try (with four dice)? How about the last roll (with one die)?* [The more dice they roll, the greater their chances of rolling poison.]

Does it matter which two numbers are "poison"? [Each number has an equal chance of turning up, including those that are poison. The choice of poison affects only the score—if the poison numbers were 5 and 6, for instance, overall scores would be lower.] Experiment with this idea by allowing students to "call their poison" (name two numbers) before each turn.

If a certain number pops up a lot on the previous player's turn, how does this affect your choice of poison? [It makes no difference. Your odds of throwing any of the six numbers stays the same each time you roll.] This concept is counter-intuitive to most people, especially since short-term results can seem to contradict it. Have students work in pairs and roll a die 100 times (or more!) in a row and record the results. The distribution should be fairly even; have students use a dice cup to eliminate human error.

▫ MORE WAYS TO PLAY ▫

POISON 6

Declare that only the number 6 is poison. Each turn will last longer, so this version is best played with fewer people. Also, scores (and addition problems) will involve higher numbers.

READY, SET, ROLL! TRIVIA

An *astralagus* is a little bone just above the heel. When you toss it, it lands on one of four sides. Ancient Egyptians and others used sheep astralagi (plural for astralagus) as dice as early as 3500 B.C.

Poison Dice

2 to 6 players

You will need: 4 dice ▫ score sheet (see page 70)

Winning in a Nutshell

Roll the dice. Toss out the "poison" dice—1's and 6's. Add the rest to your score.

The Way to Play

1. Each player has only one turn (but may have more than one roll) per game to score points.

2. Player 1 rolls all four dice. If any dice turn up "poison" (1 or 6), they are set aside for the rest of the turn. Add the numbers on the remaining dice to obtain Player 1's score. If a player rolls all 1's and 6's he or she is out. For example:

Roll 1:

Poison Control:  Score: 3 + 4 = 7

3. Player 1 throws the remaining dice. Again, set aside any "poison" dice and score the rest. The player keeps rolling until the last die is "poisoned."

Roll 2: Score: 3

Roll 3: Score: 5

Roll 4: The turn is over

Total score: 7 + 3 + 5 = 15

4. The other players try to beat Player 1's score. After each player has had a turn, the high scorer wins.

5. The low scorer begins the next game.

Ready, Set, Roll! Number Cube Games Scholastic Professional Books

13

Don't Rock the Boat

SKILLS AND TOPICS:
- Number Sense
- Number Patterns
- Compiling Data in a Chart

The Game in a Nutshell
Players roll the dice to travel back and forth inside a "boat." The player who lands in the center with an exact roll is the winner.

Teaching Tips

You'll find a simple boat game board on the reproducible rule page 15, but players can easily make their own: Just draw a row of thirteen circles and color the center one.

For a solitaire version, place markers on all of the twelve outer spaces. Each time the player lands on a space, he or she collects the marker. The object is to collect as many markers as possible before landing in the center. As in many solitaire games, the odds of winning are low, but players can try to beat their best score each time they play.

Math Strategy

As children get used to counting out their dice rolls, they may begin to take shortcuts. For example, after rolling 6 on the first turn, the player moves his or her piece to an outer space, without counting all the spaces in between. Encourage players to look for and describe other number patterns.

From each space in the boat, have students list the number or numbers needed to land in the center. Make a chart of the data. *Which spaces are the best ones to be on—those closer to the center or farther away? Or are all the spaces equally good? What's special about rolling a 12?* [It will win the game on the first roll but can never win after the first roll.]

Example: based on two dice

Distance from Center	Number Needed to Win
1	1, 11
2	2, 10
3	3, 9
4	4, 8
5	5, 7
6	6

The most likely roll is 7; 6 and 8 are next. (See the Probability chapter for more detail.) *Which spaces are more desirable?* [The second and third spaces from the end.]

Have students play games using one die and then using two dice. What do they learn? *Does it matter if you use one die instead of two?* [Fewer winning rolls are possible with one die; also, a player will have to roll at least twice to get to the center. With two dice, there's always a chance to hit the center with one roll.]

□ MORE WAYS TO PLAY □

DANGER ZONE

Increase the number of dice to three and the number of spaces to nine on each side of the center; with four dice, you'll need twelve spaces to each side. Add a pair of "danger" spaces about halfway on either side of the center. If players land on one, they must go directly to an innermost space. (Innermost spaces are least desirable.)

Don't Rock the Boat

1 to 6 players

You will need: Rock the Boat game board (below)
▫ 2 dice ▫ 1 place marker for each player

Winning in a Nutshell

Roll one or two dice (your choice) and move the marker on the boat. The first player to land back in the center is the winner.

The Way to Play

1. Place all markers in the center of the boat.

2. Player 1 rolls either one or two dice and moves a marker in either direction.

3. If a player reaches a 6 space, switch direction and move back toward the center. This is the only time a player may switch direction during a turn.

Here's a first roll of 9:

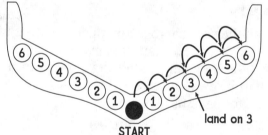

4. Players take turns rolling and moving until a winner lands exactly in the center of the boat.

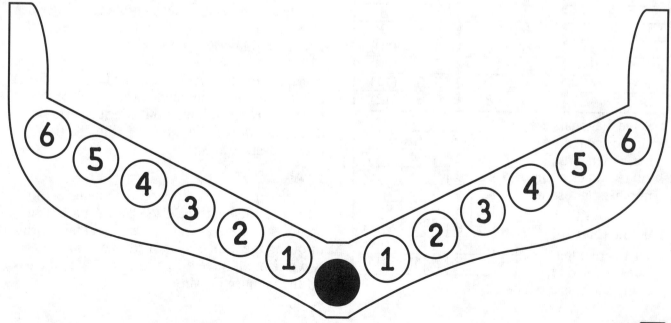

Ready, Set, Roll! Number Cube Games Scholastic Professional Books

15

Knock Out

SKILLS AND TOPICS:
- Addition
- Compiling Data in a Chart
- Problem-Solving Strategies

The Game in a Nutshell
Players roll two dice to "knock out" numbers from 1 through 9. Example: A roll of 1 and 4 can knock out the 1 and 4 OR the 5 (1 + 4).

Teaching Tips

The rule sheet (page 17) includes a sample game board. Using counters eliminates the need for students to redraw the number board each game.

Challenge children to keep a running score for all nine rounds on the score sheet (see page 70). Totaling scores will give them plenty of practice in adding two- and three-digit numbers. They can check their math with calculators.

Math Strategy

Have students list all the possible rolls and their sums (21 in all) or make a 6 × 6 chart of sums on the chalkboard. (Present younger students with the list and chart below to discuss.) Ask students to look for patterns.

- The rows and columns are series of numbers.

List of Rolls and Sums

Dice	Sum	Dice	Sum	Dice	Sum
1 1	2	2 3	5	3 6	9
1 2	3	2 4	6	4 4	8
1 3	4	2 5	7	4 5	9
1 4	5	2 6	8	4 6	(10)
1 5	6	3 3	6	5 5	(10)
1 6	7	3 4	7	5 6	(11)
2 2	4	3 5	8	6 6	(12)

- Some diagonals are all the same number; others are either odd or even numbers in a series.

- There's no 1 sum on the chart.

- There are duplicates: a roll of 3, 1 is the same as a roll of 1, 3.

Chart of Sums

	1	2	3	4	5	6
1	2	3	4	5	6	7
2	3	4	5	6	7	8
3	4	5	6	7	8	9
4	5	6	7	8	9	10
5	6	7	8	9	10	11
6	7	8	9	10	11	12

Count the number of times each digit from 1 through 9 turns up on the list of possible numbers and sums. *Which digits from 1 through 9 turn up most often on the List of Rolls and Sums at left?* [6 turns up 10 times; 4 and 5 turn up 9 times; 2 and 3 turn up 8 times; 1 turns up 7 times; and so on] *Which numbers are toughest to roll? Why?* [9, 7 and 8—numerals not present on the dice. The rolls 10, 11, and 12 don't count in the game.]

What strategy should players use when deciding which numbers to knock out? [Eliminate the rarer numbers first, such as 9. The other numbers—such as 4 and 5—are more likely to turn up later.]

▫ MORE WAYS TO PLAY ▫

DO OR DIE

A Do or Die version of Knock Out gives each player one roll of four dice to knock out as many numbers as possible. Players can add the dice in twos, threes, or even all four. For example, a roll of 2, 3, 5, 6 knocks out the 2, 3, 5, 6, 7 (5 + 2), 8 (5 + 3), and 9 (6 + 3) for a score of 5 (1 + 4, which are the only remaining numbers). Challenge children to find a roll that knocks out all of the numbers. Here's a hint: It must include a 1, since there's no way to knock out a 1 with addition. One answer: 1, 2, 3, 4.

12 AND OUT

Challenge players to cross off the numbers 1 to 12 *in order* using three dice. Players mark their progress on separate number sets and take turns throwing the dice. They can cross out sums of two dice or all three dice. The first player to cross off the number 12 wins.

Knock Out

2 to 6 players

You will need: 2 dice ▫ score sheet (see page 70)
▫ 9 counters OR scrap paper and pencil
▫ calculator (optional)

Winning in a Nutshell

Roll the dice to knock out as many numbers from 1 to 9 as you can. Add the leftover numbers to the score. The **low** scorer wins.

The Way to Play

Note: If you don't have place markers, use paper and pencil. Each player writes out one number set (the numbers 1 through 9) for each round of play.

1. Player 1 rolls two dice and looks at the number set below. He or she "knocks out" either the numerals on both dice OR sum of the dice. Cross out the knocked out numbers with a marker or cover them with a counter.

Roll: ⚀ ⚃

Knock Out: 1 and 4 OR 5 (the sum of 1 + 4)

2. Player 1 keeps rolling as long as he or she can knock out numbers. Add the leftover (uncovered) numbers to Player 1's score.

3. Remove the counters. Player 2 takes a turn.

4. After both players have rolled, compare scores. The *low* scorer wins the round.

5. The high scorer starts the next round.

> **1 2 3 4 5 6 7 8 9**

Ready, Set, Roll! Number Cube Games Scholastic Professional Books

17

Overboard!

The Game in a Nutshell

Players try to roll an exact score without going "overboard" (greater than the target number).

SKILLS AND TOPICS:

- Addition
- Probability
- Place Value

Teaching Tips

To roll or not to roll—that's the main question in Overboard! At first, the decision is easy; all players are racing to amass points. But as the totals rise perilously close to the target number, should players quit? Or should they try for a higher score and risk going overboard?

The amount of risk to take is just as important as when to take it. If one player pulls ahead, the others have little choice but to risk going overboard in order to catch up. As players draw closer to the goal, they push each other overboard until only one remains.

There's a small advantage in going first, so make sure players rotate the order of play for each round. Students should begin with the one-die version and work their way up to four dice. The target number for two dice is 49; for three dice it's 73; for four dice it's 97. With multiple dice, players may come so close to the target that there's no way to hit it. For example, if they have 48 points and are rolling two dice, they can't win outright. In this case (and in this case only), they can opt to roll with one die instead of two.

Math Strategy

Ask playing groups to discuss and describe their strategies. *What tips would you give to a new player? Is there any skill to this game? Or is it all luck? Is it better to get high or low rolls at the beginning?*

If you pull within 7 of the target number, it's safe to roll again. You can't go overboard, since the top roll is 6. But what if you are 5 away? Or 3 away? Or 1 away? How does the risk change as you get closer to the target? [The fewer winning rolls that are possible, the higher the risk of losing.]

To demonstrate the probability of going overboard, make a very simple chart. In one column, write the number needed to win (such as 4). In another column, write the numbers that will send you overboard (5 and 6). In the third column, write the numbers that will allow you to fall safely short of the target (1, 2, 3). For every number 1 through 6, ask: *Do you have a better chance of losing or not losing if you roll?*

◻ MORE WAYS TO PLAY ◻

WAY OVERBOARD

Change the target number to 10,000 and have place values for the four dice. After rolling, players can arrange the four dice in any order. A roll of 3, 2, 4, 5 could be 3,245, 2,543, 5,234, and so on. Players must arrange the dice first and *then* calculate the score (using a calculator, if necessary). If they get within 1,000 points of the target, they can switch to two or three dice instead of four.

Overboard!

2 to 6 players

You will need: 1 die (more dice optional)
▫ score sheet (page 70)

score sheet (page 70)

Winning in a Nutshell

Roll a die until you reach a score of exactly 25. If you "go overboard" (score higher), you lose!

The Way to Play

1. Players take turns rolling a die. For each roll, add the number to the player's score.

2. If a player's score gets close to 25, he or she can pass (choose not to roll). If every player passes in a round, the game ends. The player closest to 25 wins.

3. If a player's score goes over 25 (goes overboard), he or she is out.

4. If a player scores exactly 25, he or she wins.

5. If all but one player go overboard, the remaining player wins.

6. Start a new round. A different player rolls first on each round.

Ready, Set, Roll! Number Cube Games Scholastic Professional Books

19

Bumblebee

The Game in a Nutshell

Players "fly" from flower to flower by rolling the dice and adding, subtracting, multiplying, or dividing to match a number on the petals.

SKILLS AND TOPICS:
- Computation
- Probability

Teaching Tips

A busy bee can't afford to return to the hive empty-handed. Likewise, in Bumblebee, players who zoom ahead and arrive at the hive with less than a full pouch of "pollen" (points) don't always win. The game requires players to make a delicate choice between being first and staying behind a turn or two in order to boost their scores.

A string of bad luck may strand a player on a flower. If so, introduce a "three times you're on" rule in which players can advance after three tries—match or no match. You can also introduce a snake eyes and boxcars rule in which any player who throws two 1's (snake eyes) or two 6's (boxcars) gets a free ride to the next flower.

To simplify, eliminate scorekeeping. The game then becomes a simple race to the finish—without the "pollen." You can also make the course a circular one, with no beginning or end. Players compete to earn a set number of points, such as 100, as they fly around and around the flowers.

Math Strategy

Children can learn patience and persistence by using a "go for the big points" strategy. They can also learn about frustration if they get greedy: Rolling 25 (5 × 5) is a 1 out of 112 proposition, for example. Encourage players to discuss their strategies with one other.

▫ MORE WAYS TO PLAY ▫

FLOWER FACTOR-Y

Using the Bumblebee fill-in board on page 23, generate a board full of factors and multiples: 2, 5, 9, 12, 16; 3, 7, 8, 11, 13; 4, 6, 16, 18, 21; 3, 13, 14, 17, 32; 2, 23, 27, 28, 5. Players roll the dice and combine them into a two-digit number (3 and 4 becomes 34, for example). If the flower has either a factor or multiple of that number, the player can move on. An exact match qualifies as a factor, of course.

READY, SET, ROLL! TRIVIA

In ancient Greece and Rome, people used knucklebones for dice. The bones came from sheep and other animals and had four sides instead of six. The Greek word for die is *tessera*, which means "four sides."

Bumblebee

2 to 6 players

You will need: 2 dice ◘ game board (see page 22) ◘ 1 place marker for each player

Winning in a Nutshell

Fly from flower to flower, collecting "pollen" (points). Roll the dice and add, subtract, multiply, or divide the numbers to earn rewards.

The Way to Play

1. All players put their place markers on the bee.

2. Player 1 moves to the first flower and rolls the dice. The goal is to match one of the numbers on the flower petals. To do this, add, subtract, multiply, or divide the numbers on the dice.

3. If you make a match, add the number to your score. Then fly to the next flower and wait for your next turn.

4. You might match a small number but think you can get a bigger number later. If so, don't add the small number to your score and don't advance. Stay on the flower and wait for your next turn.

5. If you can't make a match, wait until your next turn.

6. Players take turns rolling and scoring. The game ends when someone reaches the hive. That person earns 10 bonus points. The high scorer wins the game.

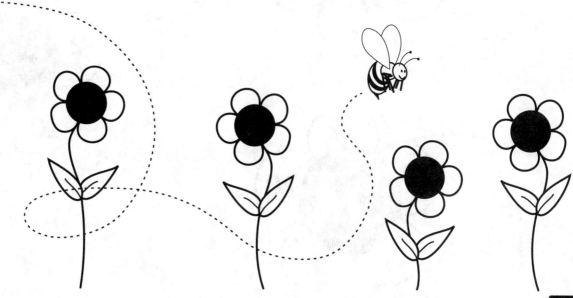

Ready, Set, Roll! Number Cube Games Scholastic Professional Books

21

Bumblebee

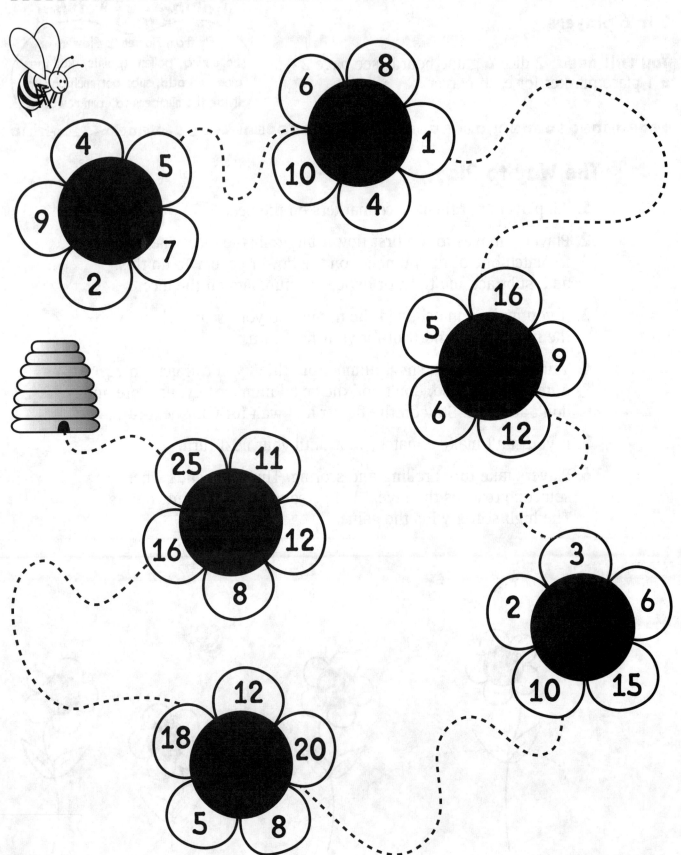

Bumblebee

Ready, Set, Roll! Number Cube Games Scholastic Professional Books

23

Score 24

SKILLS AND TOPICS:

- Computation
- Fractions
- Exponents
- Decimals
- Place Value
- Problem-Solving Strategies

The Game in a Nutshell

Players compete to make one roll of four dice come as close as possible to 24.

Teaching Tips

Basic computation is all players need to score 24 with four dice, but the game gets even more interesting when you open the math floodgates to allow fractions, percents, exponents, and so on. To give students more opportunities for proactive computation, add on extra target numbers. For example, in addition to scoring 24, allow players to score 12 or 18. To simplify the game play, players can roll four dice and choose to leave out one of them in their equations. Players can keep score with counters, the object being to amass as few as possible.

Math Strategy

If playing a timed game with speedier opponents, one strategy is to create an equation as fast as possible just to have a standby. Otherwise, a player might get stuck without an equation and suffer a demoralizing penalty of 24 points. After creating the standby, the player can then refine the formula to get closer to 24.

After just a few games, students will become much faster and more fluent in manipulating the numbers. Certain combinations pop up repeatedly. Players will discover math tricks. Putting two identical numbers into a fraction ($\frac{6}{6}$, for example) reduces them to the number 1, which is convenient to work with.

Keep the game fresh by increasing the target number to 36. *How does this change the strategy?* [Since the four dice added together can't total more than 24, players will have to use more multiplication and other methods to arrive at their goal.] You could also make the target number 0.

▫ MORE WAYS TO PLAY ▫

OPERATOR

In Operator, one player rolls three dice. All players use math operations to switch the three numbers into as many different numbers as possible. For example, with a roll of 2, 4, 5, the player can add (2 + 4 = 6, 4 + 5 = 9), subtract (5 − 4 = 1), divide (45 ÷ 2 = 22.5), and multiply (2 × 4 = 8, 2 × 4 × 5 = 40). The player who creates the most variations in a time limit (such as two minutes) is the winner.

READY, SET, ROLL! TRIVIA

The Romans named the four sides of an astralagus (bone die) as follows: 1 Canis (dog), 3 Volcanus (Vulcan, god of fire), 4 Aquila (eagle), and 6 Caesar (emperor). (They left out the 2 and the 5.)

Score 24

2 to 6 players (or more)

You will need: 4 dice ▫ scrap paper and pencils ▫ score sheet (see page 70) ▫ 10 to 15 counters per player (optional) ▫ timer (optional)

Winning in a Nutshell

Use math to make four numbers total 24. The closer you come to 24, the fewer points you earn. The **low** scorer wins the game.

The Way to Play

1. Roll four dice in the center of the playing area. Each player must use these four numbers to try to make an equation that equals 24.

2. Players can use any math operation. They can also combine numbers to make two- and three-digit numbers. Here's how it works:

Roll:

Player 1: $12 + 3 + 6 = 21$	**Score:** $24 - 21 = 3$
Player 2: $3 \times 6 = 18 + 2 = 20 + 1 = 21$	**Score:** $24 - 21 = 3$
Player 3: $1^6 = 1 + 23 = 24$	**Score:** 0
Player 4: $3 - 1 = 2 \times 2 = 4 \times 6 = 24$	**Score:** 0
Player 5: $132 \div 6 = 22$	**Score:** $24 - 22 = 2$
Player 6: $62 \times \frac{1}{3} = 20.6...^*$	**Score:** $24 - 21 = 3$

*Round all numbers to the nearest whole number.

3. Record the scores. (Or give players one counter for each point.)

4. Roll the dice to begin the next round.

5. After 5 rounds, the *low* scorer wins.

Ready, Set, Roll! Number Cube Games Scholastic Professional Books

25

Mole Patrol

SKILLS AND TOPICS:
- Computation
- Geometry
- Divisibility Rules
- Factors and Multiples

The Game in a Nutshell

Players tunnel their way to the top of a game board by rolling numbers that are divisible by certain divisors.

Teaching Tips

With two dice, children can divide numbers in their heads. With three dice, they must rely on the divisibility rules listed on the rule sheet. The game board includes the divisors 2, 3, 4, 5, 6, 8, 9, and 11. (The rule for dividing by 7 is too complicated.) Simplify the board by substituting lower numbers for 8, 9, and 11. Here are two other general rules: Odd numbers can be evenly divided only by odd numbers. Even numbers can have both odd and even divisors.

The most basic way to play Mole Patrol is a simple race to the top. Players can also keep score, earning 1 point for each triangle colored in, 5 points for filling an entire hexagon, and 10 points for reaching the top first.

Math Strategy

The two-dice version allows players to order the dice either way to create two numbers (45 and 54, for example). *Which dice rolls are "gold mines," allowing players to color in a lot of spaces?* [Multiples of 12 are divisible by 1, 2, 3, 4, and 6. Multiples of 18 include these same numbers, plus 9.] *What is the only roll that has no divisors on the board other than 1?* [13 or 31]

Three- and four-dice games allow only one arrangement per dice roll. Much of the strategy in these games is figuring out the best arrangement. Did students discover any shortcuts or rules of thumb? Or did they just put the dice together at random? For example, did players avoid making certain numbers (such as primes) or favor certain types of numbers (such as even numbers)?

◻ MORE WAYS TO PLAY ◻

NO GO

In No Go, a Game Master rolls random numbers with either two, three, or four dice. (Roll dice one at a time to set the order of the digits.) The first player to correctly state whether the number is evenly divisible by a certain divisor (Go!) or is not divisible (No!) wins 1 point. Game play is fast and furious.

Start with a simple divisor such as 3, 4, or 5 and work your way up to 11, 12, or 15. For higher divisors, the rule is to check for factors. For example, a number is divisible by 12 if it is also divisible by both 3 and 4 *or* by 2 and 6. Don't choose 10—there are no zeros on a die.

Even with wild guessing, a player has a 50-50 chance of being right. To force players to think about the problem, assess a 2-point penalty to the first player to blurt out a wrong answer on each turn.

Mole Patrol

2 players

You will need: 2 dice ▫ game board (page 28) ▫ place markers ▫ colored pencils (a different color per player) ▫ calculator (optional)

Winning in a Nutshell

Can the result of your rolls be evenly divided by any of the six numbers around your "mole"? Color them and "tunnel" your way toward the top.

The Way to Play

1. Each player puts a "mole" (place marker) in a "chamber" (hexagon) in a lower corner.

2. Player 1 rolls the dice. Arrange them into 2 two-digit numbers.

Roll: **Numbers:** 54 and 45.

3. There are six numbers in Player 1's mole chamber. Which ones divide evenly into the two-digit numbers? Color them in.

Divisors of 54: 2, 3, 6, 9

Divisors of 45: 5, 9

4. Player 1 can now "tunnel" (move) along any "spoke" that is next to a colored triangle. Stop at the center of the next chamber.

5. Player 2 takes a turn. Two important rules:
- ▫ You can tunnel only along a spoke that is next to one of *your own* colored triangles.
- ▫ You can't color over the other player's colored triangles.

6. If you think the other player made a math mistake, challenge him or her. (Do it when the mistake is made. After you roll, it's too late to challenge.) Use a calculator or scrap paper to check the math. The player who made the error must tunnel one chamber backward. If a triangle was colored in error, cross it out. It's now off-limits.

7. The first player to tunnel to the top chamber is the winner.

Ready, Set, Roll! Number Cube Games Scholastic Professional Books

27

Mole Patrol

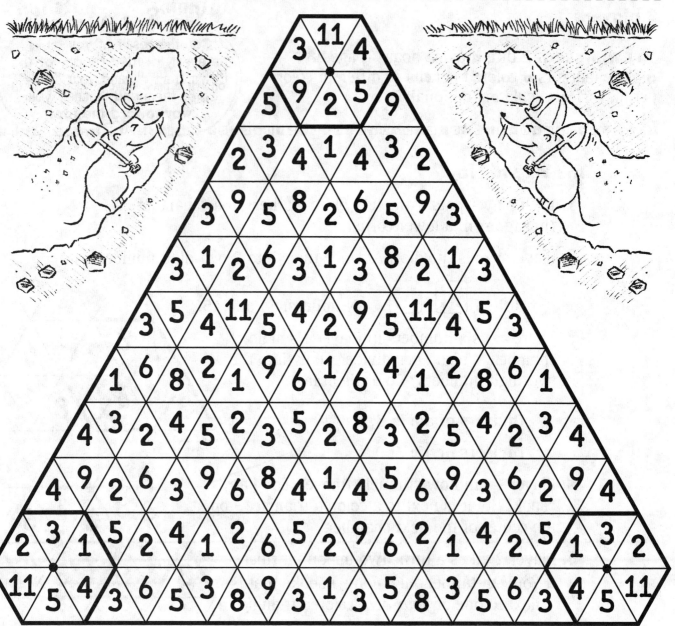

Divisibility Rules

For 2: All even numbers (2, 4, 6, etc.).

For 3: Add the digits. If the sum is divisible by 3, so is the original number (21, 354).

For 4: If the last two digits are divisible by 4, so is the number (44, 244).

For 5: The last digit is 0 or 5 (15, 245).

For 6: Divisible by both 2 and 3 (36, 126).

For 9: Add the digits. If the sum is divisible by 9, so is the original number (54, 621).

For 11 (two digits): Both digits are the same (44, 66).

For 11 (three digits): The sum of the outside digits equals the middle digit (242, 363).

Ready, Set, Roll! Number Cube Games Scholastic Professional Books

Places, Please

SKILLS AND TOPICS:
- Computation
- Place Value
- Probability

The Game in a Nutshell

Players arrange a dice roll into the highest four-digit number possible. The hitch: Each die is rolled one at a time. Players must place the numbers without knowing which digits might pop up next.

Teaching Tips

Place value is everything. Places, Please teaches students the importance of order in multidigit numbers. For example, slotting a 5 into the thousands space will guarantee a high number (over 5,000) but not high enough to win if a later roll is a 6.

Photocopy the chart portion of the rule sheet several times so that students don't have to redraw the chart each round.

To practice subtraction and addition of large numbers, introduce a new scoring system. After each round, players earn points equal to the difference between the highest possible number and their number. For example, if the highest number is 5,431 and a player's number is 5,341, the score would be 90. The lowest score wins.

Math Strategy

What are the chances of a 6 popping up in one roll of a die? There are six numbers on a die. Each has an equal chance of turning up. So the chances are 1 out of 6. Most children can grasp this concept easily, but the odds get complicated quickly. For example, suppose the first roll is a 5. Should you put it in the thousands' place? Or should you save that place in case a 6 pops up? There are four rolls left. What are the chances of a 6 popping up in four rolls of a die? The exact odds are challenging to calculate, but most students will agree that, logically, there's a better than 1 in 6 chance. With each roll, there's yet another possibility that a 6 will turn up.

What if a 4 or a 3 popped up first? Where would students advise a new player to place it? Should you always toss a 1 in the garbage? How about a 2? Should you always put a 6 in the thousands place (if it's open)?

Students can easily make a 6 × 6 chart (see Try as You Might, page 48) of all 36 possible dice rolls or a branching diagram (below). How many of these rolls involve at least one 6? [11] So the chances of rolling a 6 in two dice rolls are 11 out of 36 (just shy of 1 out of 3). With three and four dice, the chances are even higher (91 out of 216 for three dice and 671 out of 1,296 for four dice).

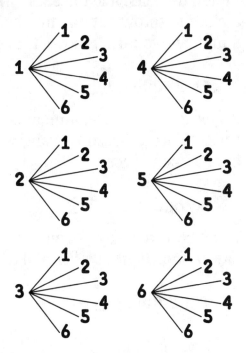

▫ MORE WAYS TO PLAY ▫

MONEY, PLEASE

Turn the four-digit numbers into dollars and cents by putting a decimal point in the middle. Using play money, children can practice making change while calculating their precise score.

Places, Please

2 to 6 players

You will need: 1 die ▫ a game board for each player (see page 31) ▫ pencils ▫ score sheet (see page 70)

> ## Winning in a Nutshell
> Place four digits in the four slots to make the highest possible number.

The Way to Play

1. Player 1 rolls the die, announces the number, and says, "Places, Please."

2. Each player writes the number in any space on his or her game board. The first four spaces are place values: thousands, hundreds, tens, and ones. The fifth space is garbage— a place to throw out one number. Once you write in a number, you can't move it. Choose carefully!

First Roll: ⚃

3. Player 2 rolls the die, announces the number, and says, "Places, Please." Again, write the number in any open space.

Second Roll: ⚁

4. The next three players roll in turn. After the fifth roll, each player should have a four-digit number and one number in the garbage.

Third Roll: ⚄

Fourth Roll: ⚅

Fifth Roll: ⚀

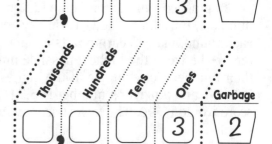

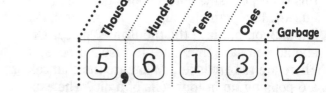

5. The player with the highest number earns 5 points. (If two players tie, they both earn the points.) The player with the next highest number earns 3 points. The player with the third highest number earns 1 point. Record the scores on the score sheet.

6. Player 2 rolls the die to start the next round.

7. The high scorer after six rounds is the winner.

30

Ready, Set, Roll! Number Cube Games Scholastic Professional Books

Places, Please

Thousands	Hundreds	Tens	Ones	Garbage		Thousands	Hundreds	Tens	Ones	Garbage
☐,	☐	☐	☐	▱		☐,	☐	☐	☐	▱
☐,	☐	☐	☐	▱		☐,	☐	☐	☐	▱
☐,	☐	☐	☐	▱		☐,	☐	☐	☐	▱
☐,	☐	☐	☐	▱		☐,	☐	☐	☐	▱
☐,	☐	☐	☐	▱		☐,	☐	☐	☐	▱
☐,	☐	☐	☐	▱		☐,	☐	☐	☐	▱
☐,	☐	☐	☐	▱		☐,	☐	☐	☐	▱
☐,	☐	☐	☐	▱		☐,	☐	☐	☐	▱
☐,	☐	☐	☐	▱		☐,	☐	☐	☐	▱
☐,	☐	☐	☐	▱		☐,	☐	☐	☐	▱
☐,	☐	☐	☐	▱		☐,	☐	☐	☐	▱

Ready, Set, Roll! Number Cube Games Scholastic Professional Books

31

Lotto Factor-y

SKILLS AND TOPICS:
- ▢ Computation
- ▢ Factors
- ▢ Multiples
- ▢ Compiling Data in a Chart

The Game in a Nutshell
A Game Master rolls dice to generate random numbers. Players cover factors or multiples of these numbers on their game board until someone scores a Lotto—five covered spaces in a row.

Teaching Tips

The games involving divisibility tests (see Mole Patrol and Bumblebee, pages 26 and 20) are a good warm-up to this game.

Appoint a Game Master (a non-player who rolls the dice and announces the numbers) and play Lotto Factor-y with small groups or the whole class. To play with the whole class, students can generate more randomly numbered boards by scrambling the numbers on the existing boards.

Math Strategy

What are the largest and smallest numbers the Game Master can generate using two dice? (By all means expand to three or four dice, if students are ready for a challenge.) *Do students know all the factors for the numbers 11 through 66? What numbers in this range are excluded from the game?* [numbers with a 0, 7, 8, or 9—digits that don't appear on a die]

The 1 in the center of the board is almost a free space, since it is a factor of every number. *How does this fact affect students' strategy? Should they play the 1 right away, or wait until later in the game?* [They can play the 1 when they encounter a number that they're not sure about or that doesn't have many factors, for example.]

Deciding which way to order the two digits presents an interesting challenge. Solicit students' ideas. *Did they find the choice easy, hard, or mixed? What would they do differently in the next game? What advice would they give a friend about how to play this game?*

▢ MORE WAYS TO PLAY ▢

MULTIPLE LOTTO

Multiples are the reverse of factors and make excellent numbers for a game of Multiple Lotto. The rules are basically the same, except that the Game Master adds the dice to arrive at one number between 2 and 12. (There's only one number per roll to consider in this version.) Players look for a multiple of the number. For example, with a roll of 6, a player could cover either 18, 24, 36, 42, 48, 54, 60, 66, 72, 78, 84, 90, or 96!

Sample boards are on page 35. To make more boards, students can create a chart of multiples for the numbers 2 through 12. (Multiples chosen for use in the game range from 14 to 99.) These are the numbers to use on the Multiple Lotto board.

READY, SET, ROLL! TRIVIA

Here's a quick list of a few dice materials from ancient cultures: plum stones, peach stones, sticks, stones, seeds, bones, teeth, horns, porcelain, pebbles, pottery pieces, shells, ivory, amber, bronze, agate, crystal, onyx, alabaster, marble.

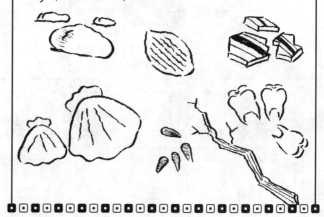

THE RULES OF THE GAME
Lotto Factor-y

4 or more players, plus a Game Master

You will need: 2 dice ▫ 1 game board per player
(see page 34) ▫ 10 counters per player
▫ scrap paper ▫ pencil

The Way to Play

1. Every player (or team) has a Lotto Factor-y board.

2. The Game Master rolls two dice and announces the number (or numbers). For example, a roll of 4 and 6 can be 46 or 64.

3. Players search their boards for a factor of the number (including the number itself.) Cover one factor with a counter.

4. The Game Master keeps rolling numbers until a player gets five in a row. This player says, "Factor-y!"

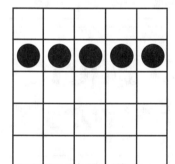
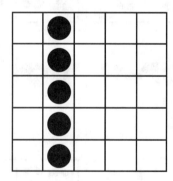
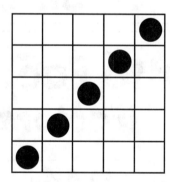

5. The Game Master checks the player's factors against the list of called numbers. If everything checks out, the player wins. If not, keep playing until someone else gets five in a row.

Ready, Set, Roll! Number Cube Games Scholastic Professional Books

33

Lotto Factor-y

Lotto Factor-y (Factors)

2	13	22	6	17
27	11	16	4	8
7	26	(1)	15	28
18	5	21	31	23
9	14	32	12	3

Lotto Factor-y (Factors)

5	31	23	22	8
7	14	6	11	27
12	3	(1)	32	28
15	9	4	2	21
18	26	16	17	13

Lotto Factor-y (Factors)

18	31	16	8	11
14	26	4	28	2
23	21	(1)	12	17
5	3	13	9	27
15	22	32	6	7

Lotto Factor-y (Factors)

32	2	28	9	17
3	26	6	22	18
27	7	(1)	21	4
16	11	31	8	13
15	23	14	5	12

Ready, Set, Roll! Number Cube Games Scholastic Professional Books

Lotto Factor-y

Lotto Factor-y (Multiples)

24	18	21	45	27
42	22	16	30	35
45	36	FREE	84	54
33	15	20	48	72
28	40	60	55	32

Lotto Factor-y (Multiples)

96	18	42	63	28
35	72	55	60	90
33	24	FREE	68	32
56	49	45	21	20
36	66	30	99	54

Lotto Factor-y (Multiples)

99	96	16	20	49
72	14	36	68	33
60	80	FREE	27	22
21	24	35	44	45
75	48	54	88	28

Lotto Factor-y (Multiples)

14	40	28	24	84
54	27	48	18	78
20	16	FREE	40	42
88	36	21	55	63
54	66	99	90	35

Ready, Set, Roll! Number Cube Games Scholastic Professional Books

35

Seesaw

SKILLS AND TOPICS:
- Computation
- Equations
- Algebraic Thinking

Teaching Tips

Using a scale or balance is a tried-and-true way of introducing algebraic principles. Without even knowing it, students "do algebra" just by shifting an object from one side of the scale to the other. Seesaw turns this technique into an exciting, fast-paced game involving four dice and a very simple game board.

Make the game more challenging by multiplying the pairs of dice instead of adding them. You can also allow mixed operations. For example, students may end up with equations such as $6 + 2 = 2 \times 4$.

Math Strategy

If players are rerolling one of the four dice, have them announce the number that they need to win. They can use scrap paper to write down the equation, if necessary. After students have completed a game, translate typical game problems into algebraic equations such as $6 + 4 = 3 + x$. The x stands for the die that students are about to roll.

◘ MORE WAYS TO PLAY ◘

THE EQUALIZER

In The Equalizer, players roll four dice and then use any math operations possible to turn the dice into a true equation. They can also put any number of numbers on either side of the equation or even set all four numbers equal to 0. To make the task a bit easier, the equations can include inequalities. An equation with an equal sign wins 5 points, and an inequality earns 3 points. Also score players on speed and complexity of operations.

READY, SET, ROLL! TRIVIA

The earliest known dice were found in a 5,000-year-old tomb in the Sumerian city of Ur. Made of ivory and lapis lazuli, they belonged to a board game that people no longer know how to play. The pyramid-shaped dice have two marked corners and two plain corners.

Seesaw

2 players

You will need: 4 dice ▫ game board (below) ▫ score sheet (page 70)

Winning in a Nutshell

Roll the dice to form an equation and keep rerolling one die at a time until the equation is true (both sides are equal).

The Way to Play

1. Each player rolls two dice on the same turn. Put the pairs of dice on opposite sides of the seesaw (below).

2. If the equation is true, say, "Seesaw!" The first to say it (and be correct) wins the first round.

3. If the sums are unequal, player 1 has two choices:
   ▫ Switch the two outside numbers.
   ▫ Reroll any one of the four dice.

4. If the new value balances the equation, say, "Seesaw!" to win.

5. Keep taking turns until the equation balances. Write the final equation on the score sheet. Write the winner's initials next to it.

6. Player 2 starts the next round. The first player to win seven rounds wins the game.

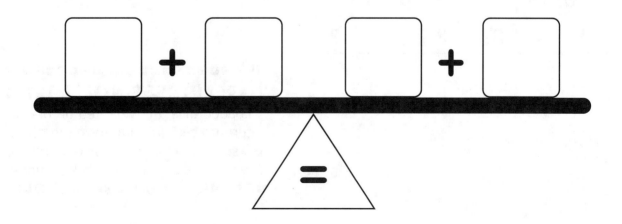

Ready, Set, Roll! Number Cube Games Scholastic Professional Books

37

Gridlock

SKILLS AND TOPICS:
- Computation
- Mental Math
- Algebraic Thinking

The Game in a Nutshell

Players take turns rolling a die and entering the numbers on a blank grid. The first to complete a row, column, or diagonal that adds up to a target number is the winner.

Teaching Tips

The numerous permutations of this game include the number of dice used, the size of the grid, the target number to win, the math operation, and whether a calculator is permitted. Start with one die, a 4 × 4 grid, a target of 14, addition only, and no calculator (to encourage mental addition of a single-digit column of numbers).

A quick mental math trick is to group numbers that add up to 10. For example, in a row of 3, 4, 1, 6, add 6 + 4 to get 10; then add 3 + 1 to get 4; 10 + 4 = 14.

To encourage algebraic thinking, add a "?" to any space on the grid. This "?" can be any number players want. It stays a question mark through the whole game until the winner uses it in a sequence.

Math Strategy

What are the possible numbers to roll? [1, 2, 3, 4, 5, 6] *What's the highest possible sum for a row, column, or diagonal?* [24—4 grid spaces multiplied by a high roll of 6] *The lowest?* [4—or four 1's]

To reach 14, will you have to roll mostly higher, lower, or middle numbers? [Middle—14 is halfway between 24 and 4.] Have students calculate good target numbers for a 3 × 3 grid, a 5 × 5 grid, and a 6 × 6 grid. A good target number is one that's average or near the average of possible rolls.

◘ MORE WAYS TO PLAY ◘

GRID AND BEAR IT

For more challenging play, roll two dice and add them. Increase the target number (for a 4 × 4 grid) to 30. Allow the use of a calculator if the mental math proves too difficult. Or increase the grid to 5 × 5 and the target number to 36.

	3	6	1
3	4		2
1	6	5	
	1	6	3

	6	2	5
6	2	5	1
3	6	4	
2			3

READY, SET, ROLL! TRIVIA

Loaded dice are weighted on one side to turn up certain numbers more often. The first mention of this crooked practice was made in ancient Greek writings.

Gridlock

2 or 3 players

You will need: 1 die ▫ 1 pencil with eraser per player ▫ game board (below)

Winning in a Nutshell

Take turns rolling the die and writing the numbers in a grid. The first to create a row, column, or diagonal that adds up to 14 wins.

The Way to Play

1. Player 1 rolls the die and writes the number in any grid square.

2. Player 2 rolls and writes the number in an empty space on the same grid.

3. Players take turns until a winner creates a row, column, or diagonal that adds up to 14.

4. What if a row, column, or diagonal has four numbers that don't add up to 14? In this case—and only this case—you can erase a number and replace it with one you rolled.

5. What if a player creates a winner but doesn't see it? Whoever spots it before the next turn wins. After the next player has rolled, no one can claim the win.

Ready, Set, Roll! Number Cube Games Scholastic Professional Books

39

The Fractionator

SKILLS AND TOPICS:

◻ Fractions
◻ Inequalities
◻ Compiling Data into a Chart

The Game in a Nutshell

Players roll two dice to form a fraction—the lower number the numerator and the higher number the denominator. The player with the higher fraction wins a counter.

Teaching Tips

Only the denominators 1 through 6 can appear on a die. Review how to use multiplication to create common denominators and compare fractions on equal footing.

If you have a fraction kit, children can use it to visualize the fractional amounts—compare $\frac{1}{2}$ to $\frac{1}{3}$ at a glance, for example.

Math Strategy

Children can make a simple chart and analyze the numbers.

	1	2	3	4	5	6
1	$\frac{1}{1}$	X	X	X	X	X
2	$\frac{1}{2}$	$\frac{2}{2}$	X	X	X	X
3	$\frac{1}{3}$	$\frac{2}{3}$	$\frac{3}{3}$	X	X	X
4	$\frac{1}{4}$	$\frac{2}{4}$	$\frac{3}{4}$	$\frac{4}{4}$	X	X
5	$\frac{1}{5}$	$\frac{2}{5}$	$\frac{3}{5}$	$\frac{4}{5}$	$\frac{5}{5}$	X
6	$\frac{1}{6}$	$\frac{2}{6}$	$\frac{3}{6}$	$\frac{4}{6}$	$\frac{5}{6}$	$\frac{6}{6}$

◻ *How many different fractions are possible?* [twenty-one]

◻ *What's the highest possible roll?* [1]

◻ *How many high rolls are possible?* [six—$\frac{1}{1}$, $\frac{2}{2}$, $\frac{3}{3}$, $\frac{4}{4}$, $\frac{5}{5}$, $\frac{6}{6}$]

◻ *What are the chances of rolling a 1?* [6 in 21]

◻ *What's the lowest possible roll?* [$\frac{1}{6}$].

◻ *How many rolls equal $\frac{1}{2}$?* [three—$\frac{1}{2}$, $\frac{2}{4}$, $\frac{3}{6}$]

◻ *How many values are possible?* [Cross out equivalents, such as $\frac{2}{4}$ and $\frac{3}{6}$ and only twelve fractions remain.]

◻ *Is it better to roll higher numbers such as 5 or 6? Why or why not?* [Rolling high numbers means a high denominator but not necessarily a high fraction. For example, $\frac{1}{3}$ is higher than $\frac{1}{6}$.]

$$\frac{\boxed{\because}}{\boxed{\because\because}} = \frac{3}{4}$$

$$\frac{\boxed{\cdot}}{\boxed{\therefore}} = \frac{1}{3}$$

$$\frac{\boxed{\vdots\cdot}}{\boxed{\vdots\vdots}} = \frac{5}{6}$$

◻ MORE WAYS TO PLAY ◻

SUM UP

Like The Fractionator, Sum Up is a dice version of the classic card game War using simpler operations. Two players roll a die at the same time. The first player to state the correct product (or sum or difference) of the two numbers wins 1 point. For doubles (two dice of the same number) each player rolls a second die and calculates the total of all four dice to win 2 points.

The Fractionator

2 players

You will need: 4 dice ▫ counters (to keep score)
▫ calculator (optional) ▫ fraction kit (optional)

Winning in a Nutshell

Roll two dice to form a
fraction. The player with the
higher fraction wins.

The Way to Play

1. Divide the counters in half.

2. At the same time, each player rolls two dice. To form fractions, put the lower numbers on top and higher numbers on the bottom.

$$\frac{\boxed{\because}}{\boxed{\vdots\vdots}} = \frac{3}{4}$$

3. The player with the lower fraction gives the other player a counter.

4. What if the fractions are equal? Each player leaves one die on the table, as is, and rolls the other die. Combine the new roll with the old die to form a new fraction. The higher fraction wins three counters.

5. Players roll until a winner has all the counters.

Ready, Set, Roll! Number Cube Games Scholastic Professional Books

41

Gonzo!

The Game in a Nutshell

Roll three dice and vie to decide if the numbers are "Gonzo!" (a matching set) or "Garbage!" (a mismatched bunch).

SKILLS AND TOPICS:
- Number Patterns
- Logical Thinking

Teaching Tips

Students play in groups of two or three. Before they begin, review the three possible Gonzo! sets:

- The dice are all the same (1, 1, 1)
- The dice are all odd (1, 3, 5) or all even (2, 2, 6)
- The dice are in a series (3, 4, 5)

For the first game, suggest that students roll a few practice rounds until everyone gets the hang of it. After several games, you may want to introduce the Double Gonzo! rule. If the dice meet two of the three Gonzo! requirements (1, 1, 1, qualifies as all odd and all the same), the winner can earn 10 points by saying, "Double Gonzo!"

Math Strategy

Gonzo! requires looking for three things at once. The trick is to rule out categories as quickly as possible. *How many series are possible with three dice? What are they?* [1, 2, 3; 2, 3, 4; 3, 4, 5; 4, 5, 6] *How many identical sets are possible?* [1, 1, 1; 2, 2, 2; 3, 3, 3; 4, 4, 4; 5, 5, 5; 6, 6, 6] The odd versus even set has more members. Have students make a list.

Double Gonzo! isn't as tricky as it sounds. Can students find an easy way to spot one? *Which categories can appear at the same time?* [Only the identical set and the odd and even categories; all identical sets are Double Gonzo!] Every time students see an identical set, they can safely say, "Double Gonzo!"

▫ MORE WAYS TO PLAY ▫

FOUR-WAY GONZO!

Add a fourth die to the roll. The number of Gonzo! sets will decrease, so introduce new ones: two pairs (3, 3, 4, 4,) and a so-called "Venus roll" in which all the numbers are different but don't belong to another Gonzo! set (1, 3, 4, 6).

READY, SET, ROLL! TRIVIA

A "Venus" roll, according to ancient Romans, is a roll in which all four or all five dice show a different number.

Gonzo!

2 or 3 players

You will need: 3 dice ◻ score sheet (see page 70)

Winning in a Nutshell

Roll the dice and see if they match a Gonzo! rule.
The first one to say, "Gonzo!" or "Garbage!" wins the points.

The Way to Play

1. Everyone plays on each turn.

2. Player 1 rolls three dice. All players look to see if they match one of these three patterns:

   ◻ They're all the same number.

   ◻ They're all odd or all even.

                                          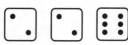

   ◻ They're in a series.

3. If the dice match one of the three patterns, the first player to say "Gonzo!" earns 5 points. If the dice match none of the three dice patterns, the first player to say "Garbage!" earns 5 points. (Record all scores on a score sheet.)

4. If someone says "Gonzo!" or "Garbage!" at the wrong time, it's up to the other players to challenge. The challenger must provide proof that the challengee is wrong. For example, suppose the challengee said "Gonzo!" The challenger must explain why the dice match none of the three patterns and so are "Garbage!"

5. The winner of the challenge earns 5 points. There's no penalty for being wrong about a challenge.

6. Pass the dice to Player 2 and play another round.

7. The winner is the first player to reach a score of 25.

Ready, Set, Roll! Number Cube Games Scholastic Professional Books

43

Good Call

SKILLS AND TOPICS:
- Probability

The Game in a Nutshell
Players take turns calling out a number and then trying to roll it with the two dice. The player who calls and rolls the most matching numbers is the winner.

Teaching Tips

After playing the game several times, students will catch on to the fact that certain numbers are easier to get (see Math Strategy, below). At this point, introduce a scoring twist to keep the game exciting. Tell players to award themselves a number of points equal to the numbers that they have called and rolled. If they call 10 and roll it, they get 10 points.

If you have extra dice, invite more players or use three or four dice (change the numbers to 3 to 18 or 4 to 24).

Math Strategy

Does it matter which number you call? Are certain numbers easier or harder to roll? Players could keep a tally of all the rolls in the game. *Which numbers come up most often?* [7, 6, and 8 are most likely to appear. Other numbers may pop up frequently in just a few rolls, but almost certainly not in the long run.]

How many ways can the dice form each number? For example, a 7 could be 6 + 1, 5 + 2, 4 + 3, or the reverse of these three rolls. That's six possible ways to roll a 7. How many possible rolls are there in all? Make a chart.

◻ MORE WAYS TO PLAY ◻

COUNTDOWN

In Countdown, four players count down from 6 to 1 together (and back up again, if needed). At each count, they each roll a die. Whoever rolls the same number as the count is out. The winner is the player who stays in longest. An optional "pass" rule allows each player to sit out one round.

Keep a record of the Countdown game results. How often does someone make it through all the counts? Do players drop out more or less often on certain numbers? Or are all the numbers equally "dangerous"? How would game play change if players used two dice and counted from 12 to 2? (The 7, 6, and 8 would be the most likely numbers to eliminate players.)

Sum	Dice Roll				Chances
2	⚀ ⚀				1
3	⚀ ⚁	⚁ ⚀			2
4	⚂ ⚀	⚁ ⚁	⚀ ⚂		3
5	⚃ ⚀	⚀ ⚃	⚂ ⚁	⚁ ⚂	4

And so on.

Good Call

2 to 6 players

You will need: 2 dice ▫ score sheet (below)

Winning in a Nutshell

Call a number from 2 to 12 and then try to roll it. The player who calls and rolls the most matching numbers wins.

The Way to Play

1. The score sheet shows each possible roll for two dice. The game ends when all eleven numbers have been claimed.

2. To claim a number, call it aloud at the beginning of your turn. Then roll the dice. If you roll the number you called, write your initials in the number's box. If not, take a second turn. You can call the same number or switch to a new number.

3. After claiming a number or making two rolls, pass the dice to the next player.

4. After all eleven numbers have been claimed, the player who has the most numbers wins.

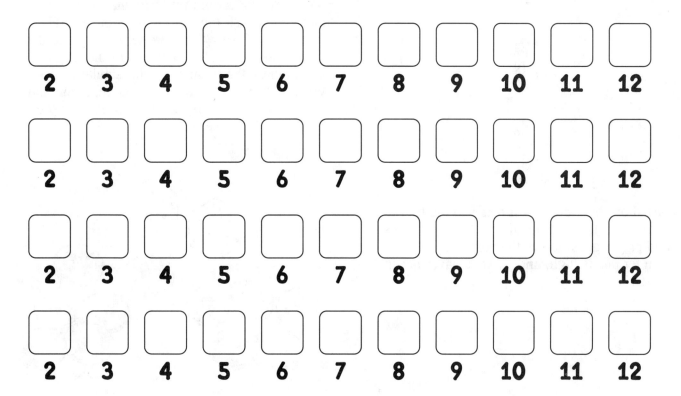

2	3	4	5	6	7	8	9	10	11	12

Ready, Set, Roll! Number Cube Games Scholastic Professional Books

45

Douze-y

SKILLS AND TOPICS:
- Probability

The Game in a Nutshell

Players alternate turns as they try to throw numbers that are less and less likely to appear.

Teaching Tips

We have the Dutch mathematician, astronomer, and physicist Christiaan Huygens to thank for this popular late 17th-century game. He called it Quinque Nove (fifteen nine) and meticulously analyzed the odds of winning. *Douze* means "twelve" in French—the toughest winning score you can make (along with 2). A single "hit" of 2 or 12 can win the game.

Math Strategy

The odds of rolling a 7 are the highest—1 out of 6. What are the odds of rolling a 6 *or* an 8? (Each one is a $\frac{5}{36}$ possibility; together, they are $\frac{10}{36}$.)

Have students calculate the odds of winning on each roll:

7	$\frac{6}{36}$
6 or 8	$\frac{10}{36}$
5 or 9	$\frac{8}{36}$
4 or 10	$\frac{6}{36}$
3 or 11	$\frac{4}{36}$
2 or 12	$\frac{2}{36}$

Based on these odds, is it better to roll first or second? If no one wins after seven rolls, the second player goes first in the next round. The counter pile is high, and yet this player needs only a 7 to win.

▫ MORE WAYS TO PLAY ▫

NUMBER RACE

Write the numbers 1 through 6 ten inches high on a piece of butcher paper. Prepare six cups, each filled with 40 unique counters (colored toothpicks, buttons, beads, pebbles, paper clips, and so on). Ask children: *If you roll three dice, is one of these six numbers more likely than the others to appear? Why or why not?*

To play, place a cup of unique counters on each number. Roll three dice and subtract one counter for each number that turns up. (Use a dice cup to ensure fair rolls each time.) For example, if you roll 4, 6, 6, subtract one counter from the 4 space and two counters from the 6 space. In the short run, certain numbers may show up more often. Ask the central question several times more during the exercise. Also ask students if they can predict the next roll. In the long run, all numbers should appear with similar frequency. When a number's counters are gone, graph and discuss the results. *If you play again, will the results be the same?*

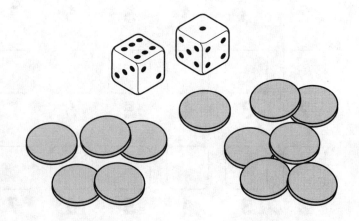

Douze-y

2 players

You will need: 2 dice ▫ counters

The Way to Play

1. Divide the counters in half.

2. Before each roll, each player places a counter in the center.

3. Player 1 rolls two dice. If the dice add up to 7, Player 1 wins the counters in the middle, and a new round begins (with the target number 7 again).

4. Otherwise, each player puts another counter in the center. The new target number is 6 or 8. If Player 2 rolls either target, he or she wins the counters, and a new round begins.

5. Each player puts a third counter in the center. Player 1 must roll a 5 or 9 to win the counters. Otherwise, players put another counter in the center. Player 2 tries to roll a 4 or 10.

6. The last target for Player 1 is 2 or 12. If Player 1 misses, the counters stay in the middle for the next round. (Take turns being Player 1.)

7. The player who earns all the counters wins.

Roller	Counters	Target(s)
Player 1	2	7
Player 2	4	6 or 8
Player 1	6	5 or 9
Player 2	8	4 or 10
Player 1	10	3 or 11
Player 2	12	2 or 12

Ready, Set, Roll! Number Cube Games Scholastic Professional Books

47

Try as You Might

SKILLS AND TOPICS:
- Addition
- Probability
- Factors
- Prime Numbers

The Game in a Nutshell
Try as You Might challenges a player to throw a 6 in fewer rolls than the opponent. The fewer the rolls needed, the higher the points scored.

Teaching Tips

In the short run, players might get lucky and roll a 6 in very few tries. Over the long run, chances are that they will win by rolling a 6 only if they stop at five tries (see Math Strategy, below).

For greater challenge, use two, three, or four dice and change the target number accordingly. Some examples:

"I'll throw 24 or a factor of 24 in *x* rolls."
"I'll throw a prime number in *x* rolls."
"I'll throw doubles (or triples) in *x* rolls."

Math Strategy

With one die, what are your chances of rolling a 6 in one roll? [1 in 6, since there are 6 possible numbers] *Here's a trick question: If you don't roll a 6 on the first try, what are the chances of rolling 6 on the second try?* [still 1 in 6] Previous rolls don't affect the probability of current rolls. If you roll ten 6's in a row, a 6 still has the same chance as the other numbers to turn up on the eleventh roll.

Have students flip 100 pennies and chart the results. *Suppose heads turn up 100 times in a row. What are the odds of it turning up heads on the next flip?* [1 out of 2, as with each previous flip.] *What if the penny had turned up tails 200 times in a row before it turned up heads?* [Still doesn't affect the odds.] The entire flipping history of the penny makes no difference. Every time you flip a penny, it has a 50-50 chance of coming up heads. Every time you roll a die, each number has a 1 in 6 chance of turning up.

Are the chances of rolling a 6 greater or less in two rolls than in one roll? Common sense says greater. To see why, children can make a chart showing the rolls that include one or two 6's. The numbers down the left column are the first roll and the numbers across the top are the second roll.

	1	2	3	4	5	6
1						1,6
2						2,6
3						3,6
4						4,6
5						5,6
6	6,1	6,2	6,3	6,4	6,5	6,6

There are 11 out of 36 rolls that include a 6. The probability for more rolls is complicated to calculate, but it approaches 1 out of 2:

Three rolls: 91:216
Four rolls: 671:1296
Five rolls: 4651:7776
Six rolls: 31031:46656

▫ MORE WAYS TO PLAY ▫

TRY AS YOU MIGHT NOT

A simple variation is to dare, "I *won't* throw a 6 in *x* tries." Players now have a 5 in 6 chance on each roll. How does this change their strategy? The scoring? Another dare is, "I can roll *lower* than *x*," the *x* starting with 6 and going down to 2.

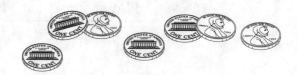

Try as You Might

2 players

You will need: 1 die ▫ scrap paper and pencil

Winning in a Nutshell

Dare your opponent to roll a 6 in the fewest tries. The fewer the tries, the higher the points.

The Way to Play

1. Player 1 says, "I can throw a 6 in six tries."

2. Player 2 either says:
   ▫ "Try as you might" (go ahead and try to roll a 6)
                    OR
   ▫ "I can throw a 6 in five tries" (one less try).

3. Player 1 may say, "I can throw a 6 in four moves." Or he or she may dare, "Try as you might."

4. Players take turns making dares until the number of tries reaches one or until a player says, "Try as you might."

5. The last player to make a dare rolls the die the number of times he or she stated. If a 6 does not come up, the roller scores no points and the other player scores 6 points. If a 6 does come up, the roller stops rolling and earns points as follows:

First roll	12 points
Second roll	8 points
Third roll	6 points
Fourth roll	3 points
Fifth roll	2 points
Sixth roll	1 point

6. For the next round, Player 2 goes first. Play to 50 points.

Sample Game:
Player 1: "I can throw a 6 in six tries."
Player 2: "I can throw a 6 in five tries."
Player 1: "I can throw a 6 in four tries."
Player 2: "Try as you might."

Player 1 rolls the die. On the third roll, a 6 appears. The player stops rolling and earns 6 points. The round ends.

Ready, Set, Roll! Number Cube Games Scholastic Professional Books

49

Miner's Luck

The Game in a Nutshell

Players roll to earn as many "diamonds" (dots on the die) as possible, but lose their earnings if they roll a 6.

SKILLS AND TOPICS:
- Computation
- Probability
- Risk Assessment

Teaching Tips

Miner's Luck is about good and bad risks. Think of a fox who goes into a henhouse to steal an egg. On each trip, the fox risks being caught by the farmer. How many eggs should the fox steal? In Miner's Luck, players use probability to answer a similar question. They roll as many times as they like to accumulate "diamonds." But on each roll, they risk rolling a disastrous 6.

After children play, ask: *What strategies did you follow to increase your chances of winning? How many rolls should a player safely take?* [The only safe roll is the first roll, when the player has nothing to lose.]

Math Strategy

Miner's Luck is part luck and part skill. Knowing probability helps students to make smart choices about when to quit and when to keep rolling. For every role, players have a 1 out of 6 chance of rolling a 6 (and a 1 out of 36 chance of rolling two 6's). These odds stay constant throughout the game.

Skill can still take a backseat to luck, since there's no way to know *when* you'll roll a 6. It might come up on the first roll; it might not come up for 10 rolls. *Suppose you collect a lot of diamonds on the first two rolls. How does this affect your level of risk? Should it affect the number of rolls? How?* [The more diamonds you earn early in your turn, the more you have to lose.]

If another player is way ahead, how does this affect your strategy? How can you catch up? [You have no choice but to take more risk and rely more on luck.] *What if you are way ahead? What's a good game strategy?* [Why risk it? Just make one roll per turn.]

▫ MORE WAYS TO PLAY ▫

CHIPPEWA FUN AND GAMES

The Chippewa, among other Native American tribes, played The Moccasin Game. Here is one version: Each player begins with 10 counters. (The Chippewa used sticks.) Player 1 secretly hides four dice (the Chippewa used bullets) in four identical bags or cups.

Player 2 chooses a bag. If it contains the red die, he or she pays Player 1 one counter, and the next round starts. Otherwise, player 2 chooses another bag. This time, picking the red die costs two counters. If the red die is still hidden, player 2 makes a third choice. If the red die is in this bag, Player 1 pays Player 2 *four* counters. Otherwise, Player 2 pays Player 1 four counters.

Players keep playing rounds until one player has all the counters. *Is it better to be the hider or the guesser? Should you choose the bags in a different order each time, the same order, or does it matter?* [Again, previous outcomes don't affect current chances.]

Miner's Luck

2 to 6 players

You will need: 2 dice ▫ score sheet (page 70) ▫ scrap paper or pencil

Winning in a Nutshell

Roll the dice to mine "diamonds." But the number 6 turns your luck sour. Roll double 6's and you'll lose it all!

The Way to Play

1. Player 1 keeps rolling two dice to "mine diamonds" (score points). If either die comes up 6, skip to rule 3. Otherwise, each dot on the dice is worth 1 diamond (point). For example, a roll of 2 and 1 is worth 3 diamonds.

2. Keep score for the current turn on scrap paper. Player 1 can quit rolling and end the turn at any time. When the turn ends, write the total number of diamonds earned on the score sheet.

3. If a 6 pops up on either die, the turn ends right away—even if it's the first roll. If one 6 is showing, the player loses all the "diamonds" (points) mined *on that turn*. (The points on the score sheet are safe.) Two 6's mean the player loses *everything;* his or her score drops to 0.

4. Players take turns rolling the dice and earning diamonds. The winner is the first player to earn 100 diamonds.

Ready, Set, Roll! Number Cube Games Scholastic Professional Books

51

Classic Dice Baseball

SKILLS AND TOPICS:
- Simple Addition
- Probability

The Game in a Nutshell

Players take turns rolling the dice to advance their batters and runners on a baseball diamond game board.

Teaching Tips

Dozens of dice baseball games have materialized over the decades. Some have elaborate "diamonds" with very long lists of dice rolls (each roll dictates an event, such as a hit), but they all follow the basic rules of baseball. Review these rules for students who are not familiar with the game.

You may also want to introduce a "mercy rule": If one player goes ahead by 10 runs, the game is over.

Each team (or player) needs a unique set of markers. Some games use baseball cards as players, which is possible if you enlarge the diamond, but you can use anything small and durable such as buttons, dried beans, beads, and so on.

You can simplify this game by using one die and assigning the following outcomes: 1 = single, 2 = double, 3 = triple, 4 = home run, 5 = fly out (all runners advance a base), 6 = ground out (runners are out, too). Though not as realistic, this simpler version is fun and easy to play.

Math Strategy

How do the odds in this dice game compare to real baseball odds? Have students calculate the odds for each dice roll, using a chart of possible two-dice rolls. (See Try as You Might, page 48.) A set of baseball cards or a baseball statistic book has data about hits, walks, wild pitches, and so on.

□ MORE WAYS TO PLAY □

DICE HOOPS

Challenge children to invent their own dice sports game: figure skating or diving (rolls could stand for decimal scores); hockey, football, soccer, and so on. Evaluate games based on how well the inventors used probability to simulate the real game.

Here's a sample for dice basketball values. Can students improve or expand it?

2 Technical foul (lose a turn)

3 Score three points

4 Defensive foul (roll two times; a 6, 7, or 8 scores 1 point)

5 Score three points

6 Offensive foul (lose possession of the dice)

7 Score two points

8 Defensive foul (roll two times; a 6, 7, or 8 scores 1 point)

9 Score two points

10 Jump ball (higher roller takes possession)

11 Traveling (lose possession of the dice)

12 Steal! (lose possession of the dice)

Classic Dice Baseball

2 players or teams

You will need: 4 dice: red, green, yellow, and white
▫ game board (page 54) ▫ 15 A team counters
▫ 15 B team markers

Winning in a Nutshell

As in real baseball, you advance around the bases to score runs.

The Way to Play

1. The green and red dice keep track of innings (turns). Place the green one on the Innings space on the board so that the 1 faces up. Switch it to the next highest number after *both* teams have had a chance to bat. After the sixth inning use the red die to form a sum with the green die.

2. Player 1 bats first. For each at bat, place a counter in the batter's box and roll the yellow and the white dice. Add the two numbers and look at the Outcomes chart to see what happens:

▫ If it's a hit, a walk, or a wild pitch, place the player counter on base.

▫ If you have runners, follow the runners' instructions on the chart.

▫ If your player is out, place the player counter in an Out box.

▫ If a runner scores, mark the run on the scoreboard.

3. Player 1 sends players to bat until the third out is made. He or she then clears the players from the field.

4. After the third out, Player 2 goes to bat. After player 2 makes three outs, the inning is over. (Advance the green die one number.)

5. Players bat nine innings. The team with the higher score wins. If teams are tied, play extra innings until the game has been decided.

Ready, Set, Roll! Number Cube Games Scholastic Professional Books

53

Classic Dice Baseball

INNING	OUTS			SCORE	
( ) ( )	1	2	3		
(use the green and red dice)	(use player counters)				

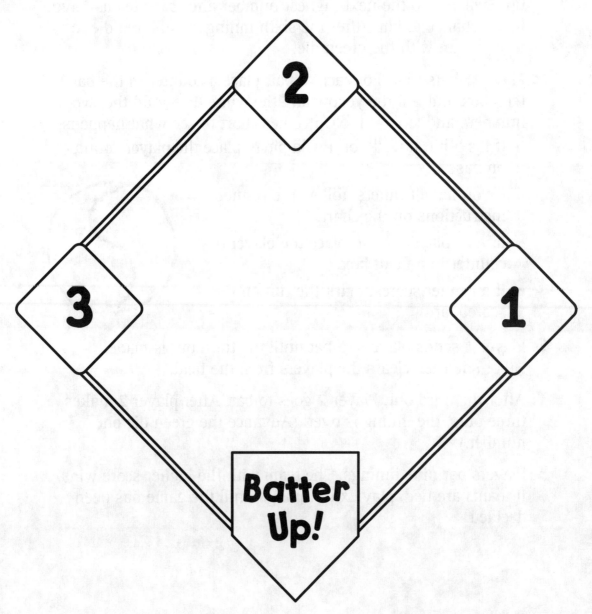

Ready, Set, Roll! Number Cube Games Scholastic Professional Books

Classic Dice Baseball

Classic Dice Baseball Outcomes

Roll two dice and add them. If there are no runners, disregard the runner instructions in parentheses.

Dice Roll	Action
2	**Wild Pitch** (all runners advance one base; batter rolls again)
3	**Walk** (batter to first base; runner on first advances one base)
4	**Double** (batter to second base; all runners score)
5	**Strike Out** (batter out; runners do not advance)
6	**Fly Out** (batter out; if you can roll a 7, all runners advance one base)
7	**Single** (batter to first base; runners advance one base)
8	**Ground Out** (batter out; runners don't advance)
9	**Foul Out** (batter out; if you can roll a 7, all runners advance one base)
10	**Ground Out** (batter out; if you can roll a 7, all runners advance one base)
11	**Triple** (batter to third base; all runners score)
12	**Home Run** (batter and runners score)

Ready, Set, Roll! Number Cube Games Scholastic Professional Books

55

Galileo's Challenge

SKILLS AND TOPICS:
- Probability
- Charting and Analyzing Data
- Problem-Solving Strategy

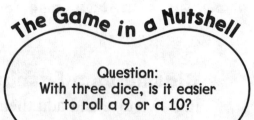

The Game in a Nutshell

Question:
With three dice, is it easier
to roll a 9 or a 10?

While not a game, this problem-solving challenge amused Galileo in the 17th century. Likewise, it can stimulate your class to ponder the patterns of probability together.

Question: With three dice, is it easier to roll a 9 or a 10?

Teaching Tips

Use three dice to demonstrate a few ways to roll 9 or 10. Then solicit ideas from children on how to solve the problem, accepting all reasonable proposals. Brainstorm ways to prove or disprove their hypotheses. Here are some questions to help children think:

- *What is the highest possible sum with three dice?* [6-6-6 or 18]
- *What is the lowest possible sum?* [1-1-1 or 3]
- *How many ways can you make a 3?* [1-1-1 is the only way.]
- *Between 3 and 18, where do 9 and 10 fall?* [the middle]
- *With three single-digit numbers, how many combinations equal 9?* [Generate a list: 6-2-1, 5-3-1, 5-2-2, 4-4-1, 4-3-2, 3-3-3.]
- *How many equal 10?* [6-3-1, 6-2-2, 5-4-1, 5-3-2, 4-4-2, 4-3-3]
- *Which number—9 or 10—has more combinations?* [They both have six combinations.]

The problem thickens: 9 and 10 have equal combinations of numbers. But Galileo found that 10 has a greater chance of turning up than 9. How can that be? How can you prove it?

One strategy is to simplify the problem: Seek an answer for sums of two-dice rolls that have equal chances of turning up (6 and 8, for example). Then see if the solution applies to three-dice rolls.

Another approach is to write out all 216 possible outcomes and count how many equal 9 and how many equal 10.

A third, faster approach is to look harder at the list of combinations. Even though each number has 6 combinations, can one number have more variations of these combinations? Try it: 6-2-1 has five other permutations: 2-6-1, 1-2-6, 2-1-6, 1-6-2, 6-1-2. But 4-4-1 has only two other permutations: 4-1-4 and 1-4-4.

By writing out all the permutations, students will discover that 9 has a total of 25 and 10 has 27. It's easier to throw a 10 than a 9!

Double Chase

SKILLS AND TOPICS:
- Problem-Solving Strategies
- Logical Thinking

The Game in a Nutshell

Like the game of Tag, players chase each other around a double hexagon board.

Teaching Tips

Double Chase encourages students to practice forming strategies. Once they commit to a path, they can't go back. For the first game, allow students to think about and try several moves to get used to the game board.

Math Strategy

On the double hexagon board, each intersection has three exits (or entrances). Because there is an even number of odd intersections, players can trace a path through all the dots without crossing the same one twice. Challenge students to try.

As students play Double Chase, do they notice any patterns in the rolls needed to win? They may discover that the winning rolls each time are either all odd or all even. For example, from the starting position of the game, list all the possible rolls to tag the other player. [3, 5, 7, 9, 11]

Move either place marker one dot to the right or to the left. *Now what are the possible moves?* [2, 4, 6, etc.] *How many even rolls versus odd rolls are possible with two dice?* [seven even rolls versus five odd rolls]

Is it better to stay close to the other player or to move to the opposite side of the board? Or does it matter? Have children try both strategies in two different games. By staying close, they reduce the number of rolls that are too small to reach the other player (2 and 3), but this advantage applies to both players.

□ MORE WAYS TO PLAY □

ODD EXIT

Have students follow the "odd intersection rule" (each intersection has an odd number of exits and entrances) to create a new game board. The shape doesn't have to be regular. For smooth game play, the distances between dots should be similar to the rolls on the dice.

READY, SET, ROLL! TRIVIA

Some dice players refer to dice as "galloping ivories." Most dice are now made of plastic instead of ivory.

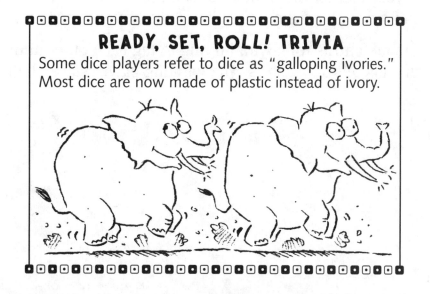

Double Chase

2 players

You will need: 2 dice ▫ 2 place markers
▫ 12 counters ▫ game board (see page 59)

Winning in a Nutshell

Roll the dice and try to tag (land on) your opponent. Each time you miss, it will cost one counter

The Way to Play

1. Divide the counters equally, 6 for each player.

2. Place your markers on any two dots on opposite sides of the outer hexagon.

3. Player 1 rolls the dice to see how many dots to move. The goal is to tag Player 2's marker (land on it with an exact count). You can't travel twice on the same road (the line between dots).

At right is an example for a roll of 9.

4. When you tag the other player, put his or her marker on the dot where you started. Put your marker on the player's dot. In other words, switch places.

Player 1

Player 2

5. What if you don't land on the other player in one move? (Remember: You can't take back moves and you can't start over.) Move your marker the number of counts on the dice and stop on an empty dot. Hand the other player one of your counters.

6. Players take turns rolling and trying to tag each other until one player runs out of counters. The winning player starts the next game.

Ready, Set, Roll! Number Cube Games Scholastic Professional Books

Double Chase

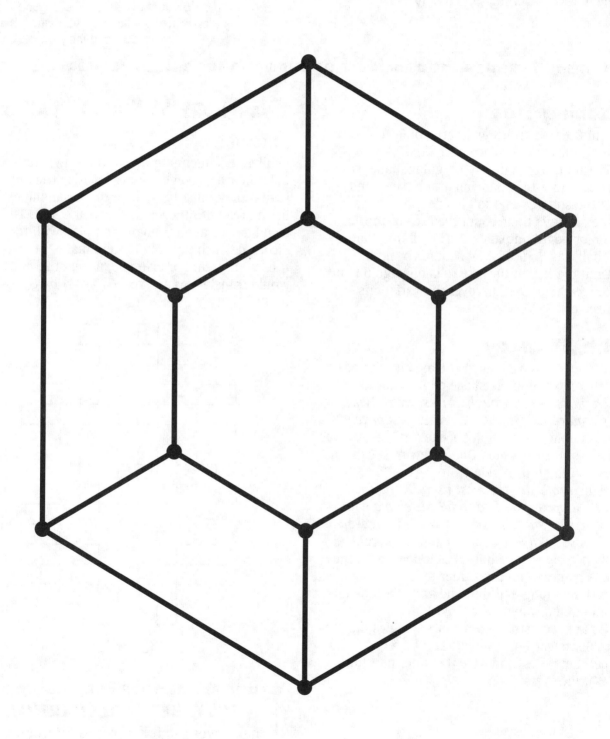

Ready, Set, Roll! Number Cube Games Scholastic Professional Books

59

Toss and Color

SKILLS AND TOPICS:

- Area
- Problem Solving Strategy

The Game in a Nutshell

Players race to be the first to color in their half of a figure. Dice rolls determine the size and shape of area they may color.

Teaching Tips

Students search an irregular area of 54 units, trying not to leave any space uncolored.

To find the area of any irregular shape, students can trace the shape on graph paper and count the squares that fall inside the shape's perimeter. Have them count the area of the Toss and Color board on page 62. They'll find that each half has, logically, 54 squares or units.

Omit the key to the dice rolls on page 62 and challenge children to discover the variations themselves.

Math Strategy

After students have played at least one game, help them examine the shape of Toss and Color. *Which parts are the toughest to search? Which parts require special rolls to search completely?* [For example, a protruding pocket may have three sides facing the outside. Only a few rolls can connect it via the fourth side.]

Which rolls are the most useful? The least useful? Suppose you had to fill the shape with only one size and type of unit. Which one would you choose? Why? [A smaller unit is more flexible than a bigger one but takes longer to fill the area. A squarish unit is harder to fit in cubbyholes than a long and thin one and will probably leave more hallways uncovered.]

What successful patterns or strategies did students discover? For example, is it better to fill in the perimeter first and save the inner part until last? Or vice versa?

◻ MORE WAYS TO PLAY ◻

AREA 108

Challenge students to invent their own Toss and Color boards, or even larger boards. The only rule is that they must be symmetric—each player fills in an area with the same shape and size. They could devise a giant board and play with four dice. Add each pair of dice and make the two figures your area. For example, a roll of 3, 4, 6, 2 would translate to an area 7 (3 + 4) by 8 (6 + 2) units.

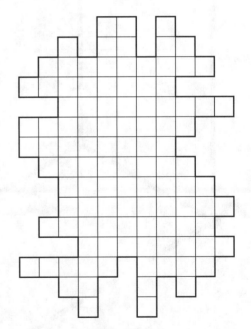

108 units

READY, SET, ROLL! TRIVIA

Snake eyes is a roll of 1 and 1 (2). Boxcars is 6 and 6 (12). What names would children give to other rolls? Why?

Toss and Color

2 players or teams

You will need: 1 die ▫ game board (see page 62)
▫ 2 crayons or markers (different colors)

Winning in a Nutshell

Bit by bit, color in one side of game board. The first player to fill in every square is the winner

The Way to Play

1. Player 1 rolls a die. The number on the die stands for the area of a space. For example, a roll of 5 stands for a space with 5 squares. The squares can be arranged in any shape as long as each square has at least one side touching another square. (See game board.)

2. Player 1 colors in squares to match the area rolled.

3. Players take turns rolling and coloring spaces. Toward the end of the game, you might run out of room. The areas you roll might not fit on the board. If this happens, you lose a turn.

4. The first player to completely fill his or her half of the game board is the winner.

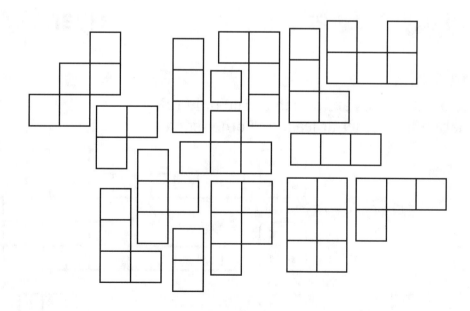

Ready, Set, Roll! Number Cube Games Scholastic Professional Books

Toss and Color

Player 1

Player 2

Key to Dice Rolls

For some rolls, other shapes are possible. The only rule is
that every square must border at least one other square.

62

Ready, Set, Roll! Number Cube Games Scholastic Professional Books

The Quad Squad

SKILLS AND TOPICS:

- Cartesian Coordinates
- Area
- Regular Polygons
- Spatial Thinking

The Game in a Nutshell

Players roll dice to generate coordinates for a Cartesian grid. The goal is to be the first to plot coordinates that form a square.

Teaching Tips

Review how to read quadrant Cartesian coordinates—the x (horizontal) number first and the y (vertical) number second. By rolling two dice, players can generate two numbers to form two possible coordinates. For example a roll of 1 and 3 could be either (1,3) or (3,1). This choice transforms the game from one of pure luck to one in which strategy (and know-how) matters.

For further challenge, introduce a scoring system. Winners earn points equal to one side of the square. For example, a 2×2 square is worth 2 points. For squares on a diagonal, add $\frac{1}{2}$ point for each line segment on a side. For example, the square (1,3), (3,5), (5,3), (3,1) has two line segments per side, so it is worth $2 + \frac{1}{2} + \frac{1}{2} = 3$.

Math Strategy

A square has four equal sides. Ask students to draw sample squares on a 6×6 grid. *What's the smallest size?* [1×1] *The largest?* [6×6]

Do the squares all have to be parallel to the x- *and* y-*axes?* Draw a diagonal square: (3,5), (3,1), (5,3), (1,3). *What do students notice about the coordinates of diagonal squares?* [They are reversed.]

Which coordinates will never be plotted in this game? [those with a 0, which is not on the die]

▫ MORE WAYS TO PLAY ▫

BIGGER QUADS

Players plot four points, alternating turns, and then connect their points to form a quadrilateral. The winner is the player whose quadrilateral has a bigger area. Wherever the two quadrilaterals overlap is the "neutral zone," which doesn't count for either player. Players can estimate the area by counting the number of whole squares inside the quadrilateral or just eyeball the shapes to see which one is bigger.

BROADER BOARD

A larger, 12×12, game board is on page 66. To generate coordinates, players roll four dice, two at a time. Add the pairs of dice and put the sums in either order to form a coordinate. For example, a roll of 3, 4 and 5, 5 generates the coordinates (7,10) or (10,7).

The Quad Squad

2 players

You will need: 2 dice ▫ 2 pencils
▫ game board (see page 65 or 66)

Winning in a Nutshell

Try to be the first to plot a
square on the grid.

The Way to Play

1. Player 1 rolls two dice and puts them in
either order to form a coordinate.

Roll:

Coordinates: (2,4) or (4,2)

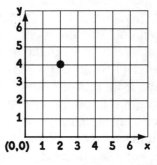

2. Player 1 finds one of the coordinates on
the grid and puts a dot there.

3. Player 2 rolls and forms a coordinate. Mark the coordinate with
an X.

4. What if the other player already has that coordinate? You're out
of luck. Wait for your next turn.

5. The first player to make a square wins.

6. A player may make a square but not see it. In this case, the
other player can claim the square and win the game.

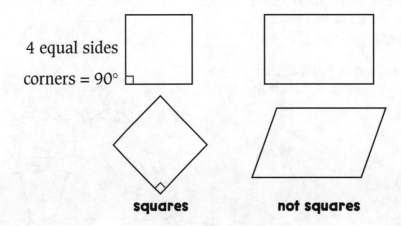

4 equal sides

corners = 90°

squares   not squares

64

Ready, Set, Roll! Number Cube Games Scholastic Professional Books

The Quad Squad

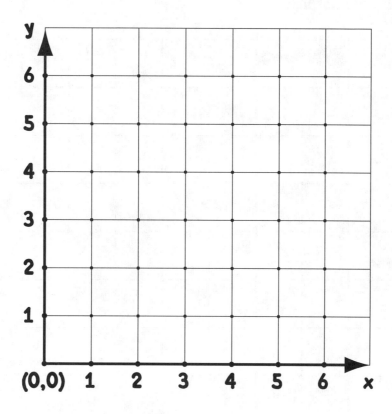

Ready, Set, Roll! Number Cube Games Scholastic Professional Books

65

The Quad Squad

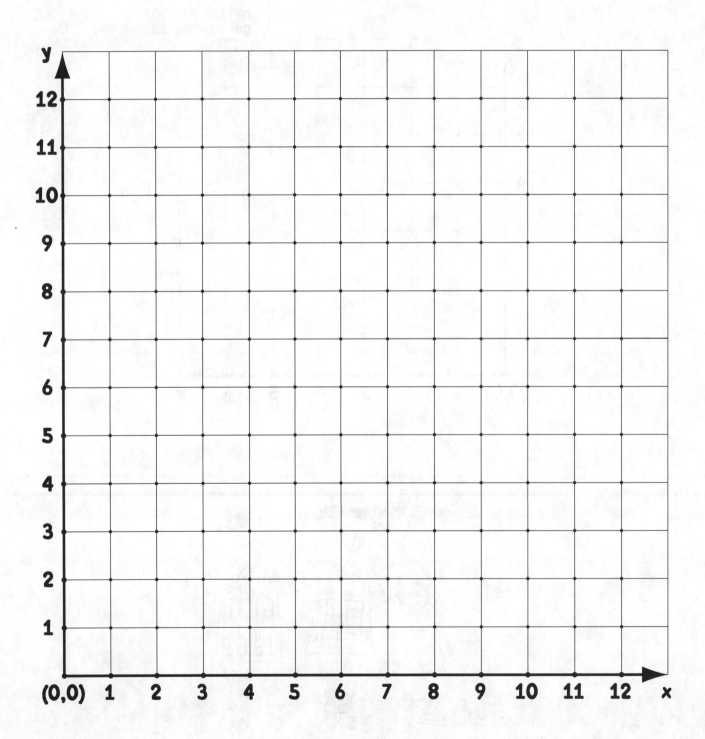

Moth and Flame

SKILLS AND TOPICS:
- Cartesian Coordinates
- Problem-Solving Strategy

The Game in a Nutshell
Players are "moths" flying around a "flame"—0,0. They roll the dice to move, trying to get as close as possible to the "flame" without "burning."

Teaching Tips

To reinforce the coordinate lesson, have students record each of their moves on paper. Remind them to include the negative sign for every move down or to the left. After the game, can they use their list to retrace their steps? Using pen or pencil, they can connect the landing points with lines and look for any patterns.

For a more exciting game with lots of confrontations, increase the number of moths per player (to three or four) or have four players, one or two moths starting in each corner, vie for the coveted spots.

Ask students to keep track of the rare situations in which landing on the flame is unavoidable. The four corner points are especially dangerous: At the start, a roll of (6,6) leads a moth uncontrollably to the flame. The chances are 1 out of 36 of this happening.

Where can you "hide" on the grid to protect yourself from the enemy or limit your exposure? [another quadrant, the far reaches, the same x- or y-coordinate] Because it's impossible to roll a zero, placing your piece in line with your enemy's protects you from harm. (Of course, you can't attack your enemy, either.)

◘ MORE WAYS TO PLAY ◘

SPY VERSUS SPY

Turn the game into a contest in which players try to land on each other to knock their opponents' pieces out of the game. The last piece remaining is the winner.

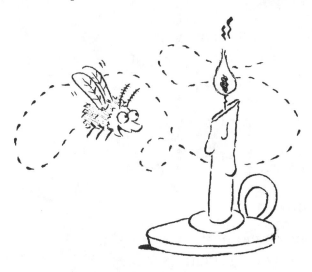

Math Strategy

What's the highest number of spaces you can move? [6] *What's the farthest you can be from the winning spots and still land on them in one turn? Is there any place on the grid that's too far?* [no]

READY, SET, ROLL! TRIVIA
In Arabic, a die is called *al-zhar.* Today, we use Arabic numerals (1, 2, 3, . . .) in everyday life but not on our dice. Instead, traditional dice have spots called *pips,* a practice that dates to ancient times.

Moth and Flame

2 to 4 players

You will need: 2 dice (red and green) ▫ game board (see page 69) ▫ place markers (each player needs 2 of the same color)

Winning in a Nutshell

You are "moths" flying around a "flame"—0,0. Roll the dice to decide where to fly. Get as close as you can to the "flame" without "burning."

The Way to Play

1. Players place their moths (place markers) in opposite corners of the grid. The coordinates:
   - ▫ (6,6) and (–6,–6) for Player 1
   - ▫ (6,–6) and (–6,6) for Player 2

2. Player 1 rolls both dice. The red die tells how many *x*-coordinates (right or left) you can move. The green die tells how many *y*-coordinates (up or down) you can move. On each turn, you can choose which one of your moths to move.

   Roll:

Possible Moves:

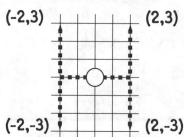

3. You can't fly off the grid. You can't stop at the edge before finishing your move. You must move one moth the exact numbers on the dice.

4. Player 2 rolls and moves either moth.

5. A player might land on the other player's moth. If so, he or she can send the moth to the nearest starting coordinate (see step 1).

6. If any moth lands on (0,0), it is out of the game.

7. The first player to land a moth right next to the flame is the winner. The winning coordinates: **(0,1), (1,0), (0,–1), (–1,0)**.

8. For a longer game, play until a player has landed both moths on the winning coordinates.

Moth and Flame

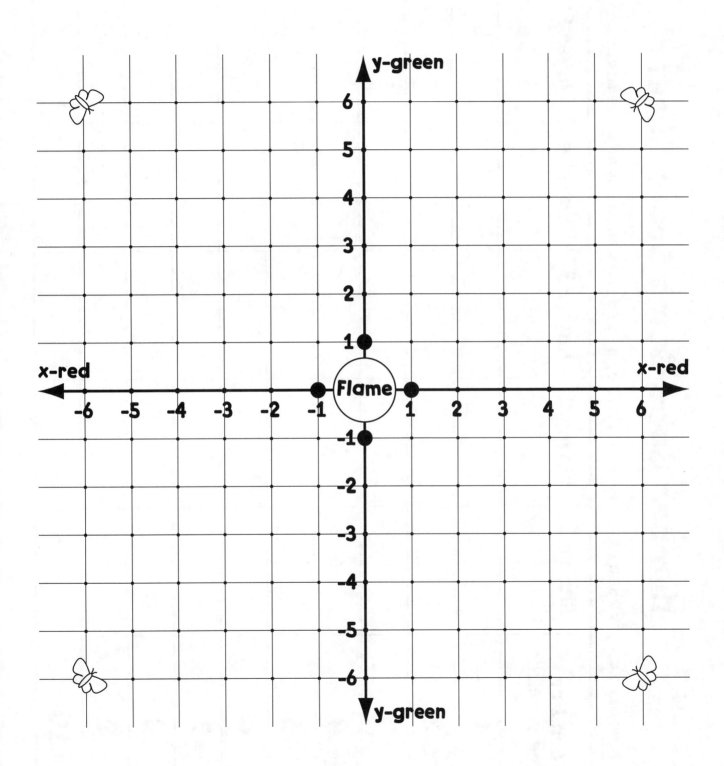

Ready, Set, Roll! Number Cube Games Scholastic Professional Books

69

Number Cube Game Score Sheet

Round or Game Number	Player 1	Player 2	Player 3	Player 4	Player 5	Player 6
1						
2						
3						
4						
5						
6						
7						
8						
9						
10						

Ready, Set, Roll! Number Cube Games Scholastic Professional Books

Notes